Why You Sh

Each of us has something special about us. Each of us has a unique vision, a meaning and purpose to our life, with which we can be the most successful, the most fulfilled, and the most happy. The discovery and fulfillment of that unique vision is your life purpose and will bring with it your highest material fulfillment.

Power is the first book to reveal how to contact, communicate, and work with the highest spiritual Power and how to make that power available for the spiritual and material transformation of the individual and the world.

Twenty years of Eric Mitchell's spiritual quest have been synthesized into less than 200 pages, so that every student of spirituality and life can find here a treasure trove of wisdom and its practical use. These are directions to find your true home, the One Power. The great spiritual beings of the past changed our socieites, but the transformation of human consciousness did not happen. This book presents a new approach to solving that problem.

About the Author

Eric Mitchell entered the University of California in 1967 with a burning desire to understand the secrets of life. He read the current psychological and philosophical literature and found it mostly empty. After a period of intense study and practice, a spiritual awakening occurred.

Two years later he was practicing Zen in San Francisco and then began the study of Chinese Mahayana Buddhism. He became an ordained monk in Taiwan in 1971 and spent the next six years in an intense study. In 1976 there came a study of Theravada Buddhism, then Tibetan Buddhism, and in 1978, a shift into the Hindu teachings.

After so many years of studying both Eastern and Western teachings, Eric Mitchell felt he had heard it all. He didn't think any of it really got to the point. He understood that he was on his own, and that it was time for him to begin teaching what he had discovered. His seminars and this book are the result of those beginnings.

To Write to the Author

We cannot guarantee that every letter written to the author can be answered, but all will be forwarded. Llewellyn also publishes a bi-monthly news magazine with news and reviews of practical esoteric studies and articles helpful to the student, and some readers' questions and comments to the author may be answered in the magazine if permission to do so is included in the original letter. The author sometimes participates in seminars and workshops, and dates and places are announced in *The Llewellyn New Times*. Write to:

Eric Mitchell
c/o THE LLEWELLYN NEW TIMES
P.O. Box 64383-499, St. Paul, MN 55164-0383, U.S.A.
Please enclose a self-addressed, stamped envelope for reply, or $1.00 to cover costs.

ABOUT LLEWELLYN'S NEW AGE SERIES

The "New Age"—it's a phrase we use, but what does it mean? Does it mean that we are entering the Aquarian Age? Does it mean that a new Messiah is coming to correct all that is wrong and make Earth into a Garden? Probably not—but the idea of a *major change* is here, combined with an awareness that Earth *can* be a Garden; that war, crime, poverty, disease, etc., are not "necessary evils."

Optimists, dreamers, scientists . . . nearly all of us believe in a "better tomorrow," and that somehow we can do things now that will make for a better future life for ourselves and for coming generations.

In one sense, we all know there's nothing new under the Heavens, and in another sense that every day makes a new world. The difference is in our consciousness. And this is what the New Age is all about: it's a major change in consciousness found within each of us as we learn to bring forth and manifest powers that humanity has always potentially had.

Evolution moves in "leaps." Individuals struggle to develop talents and powers, and their efforts build a "power bank" in the Collective Unconsciousness, the soul of humanity that suddenly makes these same talents and power easier to access for the majority.

Forthcoming Titles by Eric Mitchell

POWER: The Power to Create the Future is the first in a series of three books on Power. These books will include more detailed directions on the discovery of one's life purpose; how to create material fulfillment; spiritual powers and spiritual fulfillment; personal contact with the highest Power; and love, sex and relationships.

Llewellyn's New Age Series

POWER

The Power to Create the Future

by

Eric Mitchell

1991
Llewellyn Publications
St. Paul, Minnesota, 55164-0383, U.S.A.

FIRST EDITION, 1990
Second Printing, 1991

Cover Design: Christopher Wells

Library of Congress Cataloging-in-Publication Data
Mitchell, Eric, 1949-
   Power: the power to create the future / by Eric Mitchell.
      p.   cm. — (Llewellyn's new age series)
  ISBN 0-87542-499-6
  1. Spiritual life. 2. Self-realization. 3. New Age move-
ment.
I. Title.   II. Series.
BL624.M56 1990
131—dc20   89-13824
                                              CIP

Llewellyn Publications
A Division of Llewellyn Worldwide, Ltd.
P.O. Box 64383, St. Paul, MN 55164-0383

Table of Contents

THE GENESIS FULFILLMENT

*T*here was One. It had no divisions, no distinctions, no name, no face; it just was. It came to pass that there occurred a subtle distinction that changed the character of all that was. It became power and light, and the light and power began to divide and contract in a myriad of ways, finally becoming points of power and light.

There came a time when the power focused so intently that it lost its home and identified itself with a material existence. It became so engrossed that for a time it forgot who it was and where it had come from. But its dream will not last forever, and it will withdraw from its absorption and return home to its full splendor and awareness.

This is where we are now—absorbed for a time in our objects. We have forgotten our light-essence and have become focused too deeply in our dreams. We have stared at them too long. When our intentness wanes, we will remember and laugh. This is not our home. We thought we were home, but we are not. Our home is the One.

The mind, your thoughts, and the world of the senses are all a deception. Your innermost being knows that they are not your home. A little care is needed to see clearly, a little care to listen and understand. This is not your home, and when you understand the truth you can relax in the deep understanding that you are not of this world. You are a body of power, a being of light; one of many beings of light that make up the One Light. And this One Light is the body and manifestation of Power: The One.

1.	**POWER** **THE ONE** **THE UNFATHOMABLE**
2.	**UNIVERSAL POWER AND LIGHT** **TO** **INDIVIDUAL BODIES OF POWER & LIGHT**
3.	**PHYSICAL WORLD**

The three levels of existence

This universe has three levels of existence. The first is the One, the undescribable and the unfathomable. This is the highest realm of all religious and mystical traditions, where space and time and words have no meaning. It is the highest point of spiritual evolution. This is our goal.

The second level of existence extends from the One's manifestation as unbounded universal power and light, through a multitude of contractions and divisions, all the way to the appearance of individualized bodies of power and light. The unfathomable One is the ultimate source of the individual bodies of power and light, which appear as fragments of that universal power and light. They are drops of light in the great ocean of power and light. Your essence is one of these focal points in an eternal light matrix, a descent and contraction from undifferentiated light, through hierarchical differentiations and distinctions, to the creation of seemingly separate bodies of power and light at an individual level. This type of corporeal existence is the characteristic of the second level of existence.

The third level of existence is the physical world. This is the level of consciousness in which you feel yourself existing as a human body in a physical world—a place filled with trouble, where you live out your life totally unaware of anything deeper and more profound. The world as it is has nothing wrong, but your trouble begins when you deny the power and intelligence that is your essence and hold firmly to the view that all you are is a physical body in a physical world.

FULFILLMENT

We have two main goals. One is our highest spiritual fulfillment, and the other is our highest material fulfillment. We contact and commune with the highest spiritual Power in the universe to begin our spiritual fulfillment, and then we use that spiritual Power to discover and create our highest material fulfillment.

In my spiritual quest, the highest spiritual Power contacted me and asked me to teach people how to communicate with it, so that they could begin their spiritual quest. Whenever I trained someone, that supreme Power would create a spiritual emanation, an embodiment of its power, to accompany that person as a teacher and a friend. This embodiment of Power that is given to you, which is your teacher and your friend, is the gateway to your highest spiritual and material fulfillment.

Each of us has something special about us. Each of us has a unique vision, a meaning and purpose to our life, in which we can be the most successful, the most fulfilled, and the most happy. The discovery and fulfillment of that unique vision is your life purpose and will bring about your highest material fulfillment. When the highest Power creates an emanation and embodi-

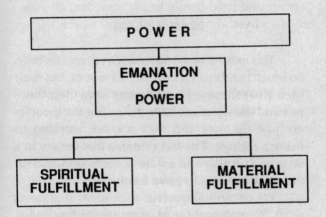

ment to be your spiritual teacher, that emanation will give you your life purpose, and it will give you the wisdom and power to create that future.

This is our quest—to contact and commune with the highest spiritual power, to ascend to the highest spiritual heights, and to use the wisdom and spiritual power that we gain to discover and create our unique personal vision, our highest life purpose. Then we have done our job. We have done what we came here to do.

REAL SUCCESS

You may have wondered why there has been so much trouble in the world. Everyone has their idea, their theory. The religions have their theories and the scientists have theirs. But the theories are just theories and they are not working to bring a change. The fact remains that we are in a state of darkness and a state of confusion, and no one really seems to have a solution.

We console ourselves with ideas that don't work. *With a thought or an image, we think we understand the world.* With a new idea, we feel as if we know something and have more control; with a new belief, we feel that we have changed. But a new thought or image in our brain will not change our fundamental nature.

Your brain is a mechanical device and doesn't have any more intelligence than a lawn mower or a computer. A mechanical device, no matter how sophisticated, is not going to have the required intelligence or power to understand and change your life. Your thoughts are no more than your brain imitating the sound of your speech. When you think, you are just talking to yourself. Your thoughts are either your memories or your hopes for the future, and they possess neither wisdom nor power.

You can use your thoughts to change the physical world, but your fundamental nature is not physical. It cannot be changed with a new belief. Your ideas may make you feel as if you really know something, but they are just covering your fear. New ideas have brought amazing change and control of the physical world, but we don't have either the power or the intelligence to solve the problems of life.

When you look through history, you see a species struggling and destroying itself in wars to solve some perceived problem. And when you look at what happened, millions of people died for some fantastic religious or political dream.

If each of us had real intelligence (not some belief or idea read in a book or heard from a learned man), and if each of us had penetrating insight and wisdom into our own life so that we wouldn't be confused or frightened, we could certainly create a more beautiful world. If we could understand the depths of our lives with great wisdom, fulfill our purpose as human beings, and not react with the fear and violence of an animal, certainly this world would be a garden.

In the history of the human race there are many examples of beings with real intelligence. Great beings have walked the earth and possessed great wisdom. They communicated with the highest Power in the universe, but none of them made it possible for the ordinary person to talk or commune with the supreme Power. Throughout time this skill has remained a mystery, and the few that have had the skill either kept the secret to themselves or didn't know quite how they got it. Many used their power to become great leaders, but did not or could not teach their skill. They did not share either their power or their techniques, and humanity did not change. We should share the power and make humanity great.

Our spiritual fulfillment is to recognize our true spiritual nature, our limitless power and light. We want to break through the barrier of fear and contraction that makes this world seem unsatisfactory, and experience once again our limitless spiritual source. We want to communicate and commune with the highest spiritual Power and transform ourselves into spiritually perfected beings. We want to live as enlightened beings in the bliss and the freedom of the highest.

Our material fulfillment is to commune with Power and to discover the truth of our life. We all have a magnificent uniqueness—our life's purpose, something that we came here to do, that the highest Power wants you to do. Each of us can possess the spiritual power to create this highest future and the highest future of mankind. It's the power for you to become the best that you can possibly be with the highest wisdom and intelligence available. This is your path to real fulfillment, and when you use your power to discover and create your perfect future the universe will support you, and you cannot fail.

Power is not like anything else. You have to give it away for it to grow, and we want it to grow and fill the earth. The emanation of Power that you are given is your flame of truth; it will ignite the hearts of others and the whole earth will become a paradise. Each person will understand his own life, what his purpose is, and how he is going to create it. As people fulfill themselves, the human race will be fulfilled.

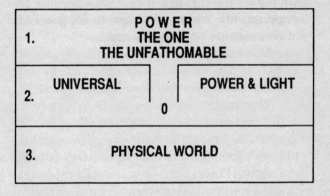

The three levels of existence and the emanation of Power

Here is a diagram showing how the emanation of Power is created within the three levels of existence. Power, the unfathomable One, the first level of existence, emanates an embodiment of itself into the second level, the realm of power and light. This emanation of Power appears as a member of the realm of power and light—the second level of existence—but in reality that emanation does not have the limited consciousness of that level of existence. It does not involve itself in time and space and is not an entity as we know it.

The emanation of Power is more of a function or an event than an entity. It is here for your benefit. It has a mission: to teach and to instill us with higher intelligence. It emanates because of an opportunity. Without the opportunity it would not emanate, so listen and be open.

FEAR AND CONTRACTION

The world of power and light, the physical world, and the entire unconscious, subconscious, and conscious states all spring from the contraction of power that is your true nature (see illustration, page 12). From the human side of life you will experience the contraction as fear, and from the spiritual side of existence you'll just see contraction, with the emotional reaction of fear not occurring at all. From one point of view, you just see a contraction of the power and light, and from the other point of view you experience fear. Your fear and contraction are like two sides of the same coin. They are two different ways of looking at the same thing. Either way, you lose your wisdom and you lose your power. You descend from the light of wisdom into the darkness of fear.

The contraction has produced a state

1.	**P O W E R** **THE ONE** **THE UNFATHOMABLE**
2.	**C O N T R A C T I O N** **UNIVERSAL POWER & LIGHT**
3.	**F E A R** **PHYSICAL WORLD**

Fear and contraction and the three levels of existence

of entrapment, where you only know your body and mind. You are unaware of your universal light because your essence has limited itself to an identification with a mechanical process: the body and mind. We think we are this body and mind, but they are just mechanical processes without any power or light. Your preoccupation with the mechanism has produced a dim state of awareness. When you stare at something for a long time, the mind grows rather dull and narrow; and if you stare too long, you forget who you are. You feel as if you are the object you are looking at. When you stare somewhere else, you suddenly feel more awake and alert.

It is the same with your Power. It has stared at and illumined this physical frame for too long and it has lost all track of who and what it really is. You know yourself as a physical being and you use your body and mind to act. Your deepest dreams continue to be unfulfilled because your dreams are far beyond the capabilities of your physical power. Your dreams are reminders from a deeper source. They keep calling you back to your enlightened state, where the highest wisdom and the power of creation are a natural fact.

As you seek to regain your lost heritage, you must confront and do battle with the two-headed dragon of Fear and Contraction. In the battle for power, you must know whose side you are on. If you are caught up in the fear, you fight for your fear. You must realize and admit that if you are motivated by fear, then you are a part of the dragon's army. When you know that your thoughts are based on fear and you decide not to continue, you have joined the soldiers of light and have begun your spiritual growth.

The experience of pain is one of the strongest causes of fear. When you experience pain you become afraid and start using your mind to find a way out. You start thinking seriously. Your fear of pain brings a certain knowledge, because you want to know how to escape. The pain is remembered, the memory causes habitual thoughts and actions, and these habits dominate how you live your life. When fear causes you to form behavior patterns, those patterns become walls, and you live your life as if trapped and powerless. You live your life like a plant in a flower pot. If the plant were in the forest, it would eventually fill the forest with the beauty and fragrance of a million flowers. If fear motivates your life, you will live like a flower in a small pot placed on the television set, with a few plastic flowers stuck into the soil beside you to make you seem alive.

Fear has deeper origins and more ominous beginnings than just pain and the development of thought. When a decision is required, there is a tendency to make the wrong decision more often than mere chance would suggest. If you search within your mind, you can see what you are doing. There is a part of your being that always knows the truth. You can witness the fact that when you perceive the truth, there is a fear and denial of that truth. This fear and denial is where your mind and consciousness begin.

First you have a subtle recognition of truth; then you react with fear. Immediately you deny the truth and shrink from it. Then you react and attack. You submerge the truth with the sound of a thought, and in a flash your brain has vanquished the light of truth. There is not even the memory of truth. This is how you create your subconscious mind. You have the awareness of some truth, and immediately there is fear and you deny that truth. You use your brain's ability to make noise and imitate speech, and you distort what you know into something false. The truth comes as a whisper, and when the truth is recognized you react with fear. Truth is easy to attack and destroy because it is so soft. We have learned the violence of the dragon fear and we submerge the subtle sounds of truth in noise.

You want the sound of your voice in your mind, and you are using it to destroy your inner knowing and to make the truth disappear from your consciousness. Your denial and destruction is so complete that even the memory of the truth is wiped from your brain. The silence of truth is overrun by the noise of the brain and is forced into the subconscious. Your battle is successful and you remain the same.

Your subconscious mind is just the graveyard of all the truths you have feared and denied. This graveyard of the subconscious mind does not exist until you react with fear and deny your inner knowing by submerging the truth in noise. This is when your subconscious mind comes into existence. It is the repository of all the truth that you are continually denying. Science tells us that we are using only 5% to 10% of our brain's capacity; when you realize that the rest of the brain may be the truth that you are holding back, and that the 5% may be just the noise of the lies that you are telling yourself, you get an idea of the enormity of the problem.

You should become aware of the levels of sound in your brain, because that is the way you create the subconscious mind. You will find that the truth will be very quiet. When you respond to the quiet truth with fear and contraction, you produce a denial thought that is much louder than the truth. The sound obliterates the truth and the denial thought changes what you originally heard into some twisted replica that supports a particular personal motive you have. The vibration of truth is still in your mind, but you have covered it over with a louder, coarser vibration. The coarser vibration, the loudest sound, now becomes your conscious mind, which is who you think you are. When you are done, you will have almost no memory of what happened. Truth is swept away with noise in a fraction of a second.

You will notice that a quieter mind is a clearer and more intelligent mind. You may have times when your mind is very quiet and still. In those times, you will sense a natural joy. There will be an openness and a clarity; and you may feel that the world itself has a stillness about it that will be very profound. You may feel a keen oneness and communion with the world, and an absence of fear, and you will be at peace with yourself. Sometimes you will see a beautiful sunset or a landscape, the mind will be quiet for a second, and you will feel the joy and the peace. It will just be you and your mind at peace.

When your mind is quiet, there is more chance for the light of your power to manifest its intelligence. But how do you do it? What must you do to have a quiet mind?

Look back and notice how your mind got noisy. Your mind begins with the very simple recognition of the truth. You were frightened by that and you denied it, covering it over with a thought that had a louder sound. You covered the truth over with something that you wanted, something that you felt safe with—a twisted version of the truth. The truth was forced very quickly into a background noise, into the subconscious, and your status quo was preserved. Unfortunately, your mind did not stay the same. It was less intelligent and was divided into a conscious and subconscious, and the conscious mind was very small and noisy. Asking how to quiet your mind is like pounding your fingers with a hammer and asking how you can stop your fingers from hurting. The trick is to notice what you are doing and then stop doing it.

A man who owns a spiritual bookstore told me that he was just a businessman and had no interest in reading such books. He said that he had been involved with this type of bookstore for a long time and was continuing to expand. I appreciated his honesty, and asked him if he thought it was a little odd that he had no interest. He said that I should not think that he was not a good person. He had his own convictions that came from his observation of life.

He said that most people who have bookstores like his are so involved in their beliefs that they forget they are in business, and that he would buy up their stores when they went out of business. He said I seemed like a very spiritual person, and that it was amazing that I might be involved with some of the ideas that the books in his bookstore talked about. He said that he believed that I knew something about these subjects, and he asked me quite frankly, "Why is it that so many people want a lie?" He was more profound than the authors of all the books he sold.

The answer to his question is that the mind itself originates in fear, contraction and the denial of truth. For your first step in spiritual development and the awakening of your higher intelligence, you need to listen and understand the twisted logic of your fear. You need to pay attention to the noise you make with your brain. If you are making a lot of noise all day long—talking to yourself—you are far from the truth. Instead of listening to your higher intelligence, you are listening to the sound of your own voice. If one could hear you talking to yourself, they would see your insanity. If you have stopped the endless talk in your brain, you have begun.

1. THINKING	REFUSES TO LISTEN TO HIGHER WISDOM. CREATES SUBCONSCIOUS W/THOUGHT.
2. NEGATIVE EMOTIONS	REFUSES TO LISTEN TO OTHERS. USES NEGATIVE EMOTIONS TO BLOCK INPUT.
3. FANTASY	REFUSES ALL INPUT. USES FANTASY WORLDS AND FANTASY PERSONALITIES.

The three levels of fear

There are three levels of fear. The first level is your inability to listen to anything true without reacting with fear and changing it into a thought that is based on the twisted logic of fear. This level is your fear of spiritual growth, it is your fear of standing in the light of truth, and it is the creation of your subconscious mind. The symptom of this level of fear is a noisy brain. If your mind is constantly using words and chattering all day, you should recognize this to be the first level of fear.

The second level of fear is seen in your inability to take in information from your environment without twisting it. When you continue to distort everything from your higher intelligence, your conscious mind gets noisier and noisier and narrower and narrower. If the condition becomes a serious disease, you will reach the second level of fear and find that you are unwilling and unable to understand other people's communication to you. You will not be able to listen to anyone.

When you are talking with someone, watch closely how they respond to you. Do they respond to your words and exact meaning or do they respond by talking about something else? When you find someone who is unwilling to understand the meaning of what you say, you are in trouble, especially if they use their distortion to show anger. If you find that person (and it will not be very difficult), you can do the following test to convince yourself that this is in fact the case.

First, notice that they are not responding to your input; they continue to distort it. Then make sure that everything you say speaks of them in a positive way, and note whether they start understanding you very clearly. If suddenly they follow your every word, you have found someone who has reached the second level of fear. You may even find that they will admit that they really did understand what you said before. These type of people have denied themselves the opportunity for growth to the point where they not only resist any spiritual growth, but they also distort everything that comes to them so that it will support their distorted view of the world.

One of the bizarre aspects of being around this type of person is that you will often say something to them, and after denying it they will tell you the same thing, as if it were their idea. They deny other people's good ideas and churn their brains until they are convinced that they thought of the idea. They will hear you say something they think is right and, thinking that they are the source of the idea, will repeat what you said in a loud voice to anyone who will listen.

Do not confront them with your test or the results. They are not your friends, and you will make them angry. Those on the second level of fear are dangerous people. They will not listen to you. They have denied spiritual growth and have denied you. They are at a very low state of awareness and they unknowingly are constantly trying to destroy the people around them. They will do anything in their power to prevent intelligence from coming close to them. Even if you are at the first level of fear, these people will be against you. How much more will they deny you as your awareness grows?

The sign of a member of the second level of fear is a refusal to listen. Not only do they refuse to listen to their higher intelligence, but they also refuse to listen to others. They have gone beyond just making the noise of thought to block intelligence. They need something more powerful and disruptive. Negative emotions like anger are used. So just as the hallmark of the first level of fear is a love of the sound of the voice in the brain, the hallmark of the second level of fear is a love of the negative emotions.

The third level of fear can be found among the severely mentally ill. Their conversations may seem like two people talking, but they converse only with themselves. They will create separate personalities to manage their fear. Those who have reached the third level of fear block all input by creating fantasy worlds and fantasy personalities.

The third level of fear is quite common. Most of those who have reached the second level of fear visit the third, and it is quite common to begin developing multiple personalities as one sinks toward the third level. Vocal changes often accompany the personality changes. Sometimes you will find memory lapses and vocal changes. You may witness them fading in and out of their normal reality.

So watch how a person responds to you. You will find that most people will in one form or another respond to something other than what you said. You may notice that what you say is simply an opportunity for someone to begin talking, to tell you what is on their mind. Begin looking around yourself. Have you seen the people who switch personalities? Are you aware when people don't respond to what you say, but respond with what they think? If you don't see it happening, you have to consider whether you are at that level. To begin your quest, look at everyone you know, and look at yourself, to see if you are able to communicate. Are you able to listen to other people, and to care, or do the things that people say and do often make you angry? Are you are willing to give other people your time and energy, or are you just concerned with the tremendous noise in your head?

You say to someone, "It's a beautiful day, isn't it?" And they respond by saying, "This car is incredible!" What happened? You were making friendly contact with someone, who responded by saying something that would point your attention to them and their possessions. This is a very simple example of a bigger problem. If the conversation ended there, it would be dismissed as nothing. If it went on for half an hour, you would have a disturbed mind, one that made so much noise that it drowned out other people's communications. Not only would you be denying your own inner truth, but you would also be denying other's communications to you.

It may be helpful to look at how hearing takes place in order to understand the problem more fully. Before you become conscious of something, your mind has to repeat it. You should experiment with this to see it happen. The repetition is very fast and is totally subconscious to most people. When somebody says something to you, it is recognized and stored almost subconsciously, and when you try and understand what is said, you very quickly repeat the information in your mind. This is where your fear and contraction takes its toll.

To know anything, you repeat the experience with a thought; the thought gives you the feeling of being conscious. When you repeat, you distort and you feel aware. You are not aware of the distortion because you only feel conscious and in control after the repetition. The repetition takes place within the contraction of the mind and gives you the feeling of the separate "you."

When someone says something to you, there is a deep recognition of it. You have already developed a fear/contraction habit that makes it very difficult for you to listen. Your fear habit insists that people pay attention to you. If you must pay attention to them, you become afraid and dislike them. So you have a deep recognition of them saying something friendly to you, and you are nervous. Which way will it go? Naturally you don't respond to what they said. You didn't even hear it; what you repeated in your mind was that "they are paying attention to me, they are there to benefit me." You respond with what is on your mind, drawing their attention to you.

So we have these levels of fear that are characterized by an inability to listen, to take in information and grow. In the first case, there is an inability to listen to one's own higher intelligence, and in the second there is an inability to listen to other people. In the third case almost all input is blocked by fantasy personalities and fantasy worlds. In all cases the incoming information is distorted and changed into a self-centered thought. The three levels of fear have become chronic conditions that are causing a weakened state of intelligence. They are a self-inflicted, self-perpetuating mental and spiritual debilitation.

There is a beautiful quote from Jesus:

> "And this is the judgment, that light has come into the world and yet men have loved darkness more than light, because their works were evil. For everyone who does detestable things hates the light, and he does not come into the light because his works cannot be covered. But he who does truthful things comes to the

light so that his works may be known, that they are done through God."

This is the crux of the problem. This is why you are here, and why you do not spiritually advance. It is the reason you do not listen to another's true words, and it is the reason we do not listen to the truth that is our very essence. Your essence is the power and light of truth, and it has the ability to come into the world. It is being prevented because "men have loved the darkness more than light." Jesus' quote says we prefer the darkness because our deeds are evil. These are very strong words, a condemnation. When we look at people who are not listening and look closely at what they are doing, we uncover the fact that their deeds are just as Jesus said—evil.

Here is a very common example of the pattern of fear in a mild form: someone who is always contemplating a new career path. They have lived on welfare and parental help for many years. When they tell you about their newest future occupation, it sounds good. They are perfectly capable of doing it because they are very creative and intelligent. After they have outlined their dream, and you agree that it is a good idea and point out that now they need to contact so-and-so for help, they either change the subject or agree with you and then change the subject. Either way, nothing happens. Nothing ever happens if they might have to do something.

As long as they are talking, they are in control and nothing can go wrong, so there is no fear. As soon as they have to listen, they are suddenly frightened. You accept what they say as true and think they are serious. When you showed them an obvious direction for taking action, they changed the subject. The truth for them is that they want to be supported; and any other idea is a threat.

This is an example of a person who is actually trying to deceive everybody into believing they are sincerely trying to learn to help other people and to be of service to their fellow man, to find a career and have a medium of exchange. When you watch what they do, they stop listening and functioning, because their real motive is threatened; then they cast a spell of false words so no one will see them as they actually are. Why would they cast the spell of false words if they thought what they were doing was good? Trying to deceive others proves they think their actions are evil.

We are not talking about an obviously bad person. Everyone knows them as very loving, kind, and friendly. They are normal on the surface. If you tried to get them to tell the truth or even see the truth, you would be confronted by an entirely different person. The incredible fear would not be faced, and you would have a trapped animal on your hands. The most hideous emotions would erupt, all to protect their secret motive.

They would prove themselves to be at least in the second level of fear, and in their heart of hearts they would know that you are right. But, in the end they would be totally against you, because they would believe you are totally against them and their secret motive.

Many people with similar problems have refined the technique into actually appearing to go insane when the pressure mounts. They have memory losses, or they become someone different. They enter the third level of fear and either create a new personality that doesn't remember, or invent some fantasy world where their fear doesn't exist. They seem to be very capable people, as evidenced by their incredible mental skill, but since the third level is a very isolated place, they back themselves into a very strange corner as time goes by.

The end result of such behavior is graphically demonstrated in the life of Christ. When the light comes into the world, people hate it, and rather than see the truth and give up their evil ways, they react with fear. Their fear, when pressed, turns into hatred, and when many people hate one cause or one man, they feel justified, and the twisted logic of fear has its way. The light is extinguished from the world. They destroy the light because the "detestable" things they do cannot be covered as long as that light is in the world. It is essential to remember this fact and remain aware of this principle as you bring this light into your life. You will be bringing the light into the world and will be battling the forces of darkness within yourself. When your mind, which is based on fear, seizes control, and the light cannot be found, you will know what is happening. You will have pushed it away.

If there exists any satanic force in the world, it is certainly your fear and contraction. In its gross forms, this satanic force is just the inability to listen, and to love others. It is the inability to respond to your fellow human beings with respect and care, and to respond to exactly what they are saying without radically distorting everything for selfish reasons. In its more subtle forms this satanic force is the distortion of the higher spiritual intelligence within us. It is the division of the mind into the conscious and the subconscious, and it is the narrowing of our mental capacity to the point where only 5% of our brain is functioning.

In our efforts to advance spiritually we will be confronting the entire drama of fear and contraction. To bring your light into the world, you will become intimately involved with your own fear and contraction.

A common example of fear has been demonstrated by many who think they are interested in contacting and communicating with an emanation of Power. As long as they don't know what they are doing, and the information is not threatening, they are able to listen and receive information. If it is not what they want to hear, an amazing event happens. It's like an occurrence of amnesia. They usually deny the whole experience by saying nothing happened. When you question them, they recall having done everything correctly. Further questioning reveals what really happened to them. They suddenly remember! Just a minute before, they didn't remember anything. Now they are describing a whole experience. After a time they get frightened again, a darkness comes over their minds, and they start saying that nothing happened. They can't remember. They have touched the third level of fear, in which a person switches personalities to handle the fear. One personality remembers, and the other one won't. This is not an uncommon experience.

When these same people do a technique in which they are more in control and don't have to listen—feeling as if they are doing the talking— suddenly the situation is totally different. If they are in control, they aren't frightened. They do extremely well, and feel very good about their skills, and don't have any memory losses. Whenever the information is threatening, they will unknowingly alter the information. This way they don't have to switch personalities, have amnesia, or submerge the true information into their subconscious mind.

When they are led again into contacting an emanation of Power, you can immediately see the fear come over them. Everyone can see it. They even admit it for a while. Now that they are familiar with what they are doing, they can't make contact. Fear makes them unable to listen. As long as they are in control and can alter any information, everything is fine. When they are in a position in which they have to listen, and listen to the highest spiritual intelligence, fear sets in and no contact can be made. They refuse to listen.

Then there are those who listen to spiritual power for a time and suddenly can't make contact. It is not from a lack of skill, because they do have the skill. They have reached a point where they don't want to listen any more. They may think that they want to listen, but when the cause of their difficulty is investigated, it is found that they don't. They believe they are doing something, and they are not. Fear and contraction is the cause. They don't want the next step in their growth. It would mean that they have to change. Fear causes a dark and confused state. They want an excuse not to listen and grow spiritually, and what better excuse than the belief that they just can't do it? The real fact is that they can do it. Everyone can do it. The truth is that they are just not doing it, but they won't believe it at the time. Later, when they are not threatened, they are doing it again and may understand what had happened to them.

When you look into their lives, you will see the reasons for their hatred of the light. There are so many ugly habits and secret motives they do not want revealed. They don't want to change or lose anything. They treat their ugliness like a rare treasure. They are very comfortable with it and feel it is their very essence. They feel it is who they are! These incredibly ugly habits and secret motives, and our desire to keep them hidden, keep us from listening and are holding up our spiritual progress.

If you were to become conscious of these habits and were able to see them clearly for a second, you would be disgusted. They have crept into our personalities like thieves in the night, and now, half asleep, we crawl into bed with them and hold them dearly. Keep in mind that you may come across these thieves as you turn on the light. Don't be frightened, and don't think that they will go if you fearfully flip off the light. Do not blame the light for revealing who you are sleeping with. Keep the light on, go forward, and understand these thieves who are stealing your intelligence and power.

The worst thing that could happen is what happened to the enemies of Jesus so long ago. Not only would you fearfully reject the light, but you would join forces with the thief of darkness and actively try to extinguish the light in order to camouflage your secret motives. Hopefully the times have changed, we have grown in the light, and are willing to bring the light into the world and drop our demeaning habits.

[handwritten: clear BLOCKS TO GETTING IN TOUCH W MY POWER + LIGHT 9/25/94]

You must understand the limited state of consciousness that leads to all the madness and suffering in the world. You need to understand how the fear and contraction of your power leads to your diminished capacity. We need to understand and we need to experience. You can experience the state of contraction by getting in touch with your power and light, and by experiencing the presence of your power. You need to expand your power back to the state it was in before it contracted, and then observe the contraction of your consciousness.

This observation gives you firsthand experience of the contraction process. You may not have the power to end your fear and contraction, but you will have seen it and you will have changed. From that expanded state you have the power to see through the contraction, and that will give you real understanding. It will allow you to change the way you are living your life. You will not allow the fear and contraction to dominate you. You will have ended the basis of fear. When you learn this art, you will transform a life based on fear into a life based on the highest wisdom and power. Then you and I and the world will be able to transform this planet into a heaven.

TECHNIQUES OF POWER

The perfection of power is to become Power. When you have overcome fear and contraction, you have perfected power. You have become an incarnation of Power. You have one power, one technique, and that is Power itself. Your one Power is not divided into many powers; your acts are the acts of the one Power. To become this one Power, to be an incarnation of Power— this is our spiritual goal.

The power and light that is the essence of this universe has no divisions or distinctions. Even the names of power and light are only a way of naming that which cannot be named. The qualities of power and light are not distinct in themselves. You cannot use power without using light, just as you cannot use light without using power. They are two sides of the same coin; a way of saying something that cannot be said.

When you have arrived at this level of consciousness, you don't use power as a technique. Your very being is Power, and you witness the techniques of power as acts of Power. The One is your home and your being; it is the mystery where words and descriptions stop. Your acts are the acts of the One. Power is the source. This is our goal.

Power is operating unconsciously in our lives. It cannot be understood by either the subconscious or the conscious minds. The physical brain is responsible for the conscious mind and the subconscious mind. Power is in the realm of the unconscious.

1. **POWER**	**UNCONSCIOUS**
2. **UNIVERSAL POWER & LIGHT**	
3. **PHYSICAL WORLD**	**SUBCONSCIOUS**
	CONSCIOUS

*The three levels of existence
and the conscious, subconscious, and unconscious mind.*

Nothing can be known or said about the level of Power. At the highest level of universal power and light, there are only the qualities of power and light. At the lower end of the realm of power and light, there is movement and the transmission of light. When your brain tries to understand power, it immediately tries to translate power into something it can understand. It looks for thoughts, images, and the five senses, and they are not there. Power is not something that can be understood by the brain, but you need to make the wisdom of power available to the brain. It is the source of your highest intelligence.

Your brain must learn to translate the wisdom of your power into familiar symbols before you can be conscious of the knowledge that power has. Your mind tries to perceive but only understands the sounds of words and the five senses. Your ability to translate the wisdom of power into symbols your brain can experience and understand establishes your foothold in the techniques of power.

In the beginning you are caught, trapped by your limited experience. You will want to translate and use power as if it were your mind, which it is not. You need wisdom and power, but you are unable to comprehend the silence of truth, so you translate power into familiar symbols. In this way you become familiar with power, without having to grasp its mystery, by becoming an embodiment of Power.

⟨The most lofty aim for your power is to produce your spiritual and material transformation. Your fulfillment will help create the family of Power that will be transforming the world. Your transformation begins with you. You need to find your wisdom and power and use it for your highest good. By benefitting yourself, you will be growing both spiritually and materially. You will be bringing your light and power into the world, and the world will change. Your one act of benefitting yourself will be benefitting others, and your whole attitude about life will change. You will just want to be of help.⟩

The light and power that you bring into the world won't be yours to hold. You won't be able to keep it for yourself. It will spread to others. True power will be shared. Your light and power will flow to others. If they are ready and open to the wisdom of light and power, they will grow, and a share of the light will anoint them. If they become frightened they will deny the light and it will disappear. Their fear will come because the light reveals the secret motives of their subconscious mind. If they are not ready for truth and are not ready to grow and change, they will deny the light. If they are seeking truth in their lives, they can use the light to change and spiritually advance. They can come closer to their power and increase their light.

This is how the light and power works in the world when it comes. It is transferred from one heart to the other, and where there is openness and love it grows and bears fruit. You have the opportunity once again to turn towards the light and grow, or to shrink with fear and hate the light—to stay in darkness as a withered being.

Those who turn towards the light and overcome their fear are blessed. They will be the creators of the future. The ones who refuse the light treasure their secret motives and fail to see that their secret schemes are injuring themselves and others. They will destroy their relationships, their love, and their life until they can bear the light of truth. They will suffer until they endure the shock of self-discovery that comes when you bring your light into the world.

The light will not be staying with those who refuse it. It comes by invitation, and when the light and power illumines the dark motives of the mind, that darkness disappears. The fearful ones hold these motives to be their very being and will not allow the light to destroy their treasures. When they feel their dark hoard being destroyed, they feel that they are being attacked and hurt and act as if they are going to die. The fear and contraction brings the darkness back to their shrinking mind, and in their dullness they feel safe.

Such is the slow process of spiritual growth, if you are not courageous enough to face your fear and conquer it. When you have the power and the light, and it threatens your dark treasures, you will suddenly have no wisdom and power and will wonder where they have gone. Consciously you may not be able to admit what has happened, but you still possess the remnants of the twisted logic of fear. You may deny or not remember the whole experience, even though upon careful questioning you remember everything.

One day your fear is gone, and again you have power, and your wisdom flows. Then on another day you have shrunk and will deny everything. You will go on and on like a crazy person, going in and out of your fear and contraction. You are trying to break through a level of fear and contraction that you have grown very accustomed to, that you have felt for a very long time is you. It will be during these bouts with fear that you will need the courage not to give up the struggle and lose out to fear. Fear is your only enemy.

If you are courageous enough to ignore your fear and strong enough to drop the secret causes of fear, you will be the heir to all that universal power and light can bring. Your destiny will be yours to create. You will be consciously working with an emanation of the highest spiritual Power and will be able to bring this power and light into the physical world. The world will change. There are things in the world that seem real but are just the false dreams of fear. These cannot exist when your light comes into the world. They are part of the darkness that is dispelled by the light.

With the coming of the light, only truth can remain in your life, whether it is present in your mind or in your world. The light has the power to destroy everything which is not true for you. What is true for you enters your mind in the light and that has power. What enters the mind of the average person is a fearful reaction to truth. When the light is there, the truth is seen. When there is a fearful reaction to the truth, the mind shrinks from that light and hides the truth with mental noise. In a split second you create a thought which is similar to the truth, but is rather a twisted version of it. You create a thought which is more acceptable and doesn't cause fear. You twist the truth into a thought that says you don't have to change, that supports your secret motives.

When you have nurtured the light while discovering and creating the highest future that your power directs, you will become part of the global transformation. You will bring the light into the world, and you will share it with all whom you meet. Those who receive and nurture the light will begin to grow. Some will turn away from the light, and it will leave them. There will be another time for them.

The people of the light will know the truth, and their truth will have power in the world. They will learn the art of using their power and light to establish the truth in their lives, and the world of darkness will change. A new world will be created for them. Those whose minds dwell in the darkness will not know how or why it changed, but the intelligent will notice that everything that the people of light are wanting is coming to pass. This is the power behind the truth that is your nature.

The people of the light, who are the creators of the future, are not alone. They are a part of the family of Power that discovers and creates the highest future for the world. You are part of that greater power. This greater power and light serves a higher purpose, a purpose that serves humanity. When you create your highest purpose, it is your greatest gift for humanity, and when the many fulfill their highest purpose, they will create a new world.

There are higher purposes beyond the individual ones, and there are ways for those connected to Power to benefit others. The family of Power will help end the fear and contraction of humanity, so that each person will spontaneously seek the light. This is the grand design. As you bring your power and light into the world and turn from fear, the family of Power spreads its light, and humanity can more easily stand in the light of truth, fearlessly dropping those dark treasures that keep them bound to a life of pain.

The greatest power is the power to dwell in the highest state of consciousness. To become an incarnation of Power is the perfection of Power. This is the state in which all the fear and contraction stop. Your power is no longer trapped by a mortal physical frame. It has gone beyond the confusion of the senses, recognized its source, and ended its contraction to become the universal power and light that is the substance of this world. Your power has recognized its true home, expanded to the limits of the universe, and stopped contracting into the narrow perceptions of a human existence. You have seen that your human drama was just a tiny contracted space within your true being, a drop in the ocean of power and light.

Among the individual powers that you learn as you progress along the spiritual path is the wisdom of the power body. This is the easiest of all the powers to master because it is the one that produces the least amount of fear. Therefore, you will find that it is the most worldly and the least useful for spiritual growth. When using the wisdom of your power you are strongly in control; but it is easy to unknowingly distort your higher intelligence according to your fears. Almost anyone can become an expert in using the wisdom of power. You can gain amazing knowledge of things impossible to physically know. Without fear, we find ourselves able to accomplish the impossible. With fear, even the most simple knowledge becomes distorted and false.

Using the wisdom of your power is the way

to begin your search for knowledge and power. The technique is open to anyone who is willing to face their fear. It can gather any kind of information. Its simplicity and power make it the favorite tool for understanding the world. There are no worldly limits outside of your fear, and there are not many secrets that cannot be known by the person whose power is clear of fear. Almost anything can be known.

Healing is one of the most beneficial powers that exists. It is a vast science. Everything that is considered spiritual growth can be called healing. One of the most profound experiences is to use the healing abilities of your power and light. It can actually make physical alterations in the body.

Everything in existence is a vibration, which may be interpreted as color or sound. Illness is an erroneous vibration. When you experience illness, the vibrations involved with the continual creation and maintenance of your being have gone off track. Your power and light contracting into the physical world is based on the distortions of fear. These continual distortions naturally cause illness. The contraction of your power into the physical is already a disease, and the physical problems we have are just the aftershocks of the trauma of spiritual contraction. Much of healing is learning to not contract, and the rest is mechanically adjusting your physical vibrations by using your spiritual power and light.

One of the most profound and useful techniques of power is the ability to contact the highest spiritual Power. There is only one Power, and this Power can bestow an embodiment or emanation of its universal power for your deliverance from the illusions of the mind. This supreme Power will emanate a vast spiritual presence that will accompany you in your spiritual growth.

This emanation of the supreme Power is the most important step in your spiritual quest. Without this power drawing near to you, and staying with you, your efforts will be very limited. Outside the teachings of Power, this level of contact is very rare. Without this contact your efforts will remain at very worldly levels, and you will not be able to proceed to the blissful stages of spiritual union that lie beyond your worldly entrapment.

Your own individual power is made of the same fabric as universal power, but yours is just a drop of water in an endless ocean. Your power cannot command the universal, but through the teachings of Power, you can receive an embodiment of Power. It comes to you because you have come to the light. It doesn't come because you are a great person. It doesn't ask who you are. If you turn against the light, it goes, but if you stay in the light and confront your fears, you will grow and experience the ecstasy of a spiritual being. You will know that the anointing process has begun.

When the embodiment of the highest Power draws close to you, you can know the wisdom, the power, and the love of the highest. This emanation helps you on your spiritual and material quest. Its wisdom and power are there for you as you make your shift from the darkness into the light. The emanations of Power are representatives or messengers of the universal power and light. They are the highest Power's way of beginning the transformation of the world.

The emanations of the universal power and light exist in the same realm as our own power, but are embodiments of the ultimate state of spiritual growth. While they manifest the appearance of a limited form of power, and may actually present us with an image that we can relate to, they are not beings or entities of any sort. They are not involved with either space or time and do not represent any form of material existence. They are strictly and wholly direct embodiments and emanations of the highest Power.

By calling on the emanation of Power that is your teacher, you can commune with that power to understand and create our highest future and the highest future of the world. By contacting and imbibing the wisdom and power of that supreme spiritual emanation, you can bring the light, the power, and the ecstasy of the highest into your life and into the world.

THE MIND
AND THE POWER BODY

What is the mind? Some say that the mind is just a mechanical device, and that our consciousness is the result of certain biological, electrical, and chemical processes. They say that if your mind could be dissected, every part of your consciousness could be located in a specific place in the brain. There are also people who say that the brain is just the biological side of man, that the greater part of his being is a spiritual essence, and that this spiritual essence is what gives the breath of life to the body and causes the panorama of human consciousness.

As science rushes to discover the ultimate secrets of the universe, it doesn't answer these questions; but it does leave behind fascinating clues that can lead to either conclusion. On the one hand, scientists have found chemicals in the brain that cause moods and emotions. They have found chemicals that cause mice to prefer to sit in one location rather than another. The scientists are postulating with strong evidence that one day they will have identified every chemical that causes every mood or thought that a brain can have. Will they have proven the theory that man is just a biological machine?

There are other scientists working in the realm of physics who are involved with quantum mechanics. They are looking into the deepest mysteries of matter. Ever since we opened the doors of matter and found it to be energy, scientists have been watching matter turn into energy and energy turn into matter. When studying subatomic particles, scientists sometimes use cloud chambers that furnish photographic evidence of what these subatomic particles are doing. It appears that sometimes matter is suddenly created out of something that looks like nothing, and then just as suddenly matter will disappear back into nothingness. If our material world is resting on such an uncertain foundation, it's hard to say with final authority that the human being is just a biological mechanism and nothing else. It doesn't seem that the material world itself is just a mechanical process.

What about this nothingness that matter seems to ultimately go back to and come out of? It sounds very mysterious and even mystical. It seems to be playing a primary role as a source of creation and destruction and is certainly beyond the realm of biology and the mechanical world. This nothingness sounds like a spiritual foundation to existence.

Let's investigate consciousness a little bit ourselves and see what we find. First, shut your eyes. Relax. Notice what kind of state you are in. Notice that just shutting your eyes diminishes what you would normally think of as consciousness. Without eyes and the ability to see, you lose much of your consciousness. While the ability to see is an amazing and profound experience, it is still just seeing. In our daily lives we act as if it were the major portion of our consciousness, and yet it's just a sense organ.

Now notice that you are having thoughts. Keep your eyes closed, and consider what thoughts are. They are just your mind's ability to recreate the sound of speech in your brain. Say to yourself, "This is my brain," and you will hear your mind recreate the sound of speech in your brain. You are just talking to yourself. When you think, you are just listening to the mind's ability to re-create speech. The ability to talk to yourself is not a great skill and makes up a great portion of what is left of your consciousness.

If you couldn't see and you couldn't imitate speech in your mind, how much of your consciousness would be left? Not very much. About all that would remain of consciousness at this point would be a vague sense of awareness, with an occasional hazy image and the ability to hear and feel. There is not much going on in our conscious mind, if you really consider it in detail. Yet we give our mind such great importance.

Neuroscientists tell us that man is only using a very small portion of his brain, perhaps only 5%. What is going on in the rest of the brain? Some scientists say that if we could use more of the brain at a conscious level, greater levels of intelligence would result. Greater intelligence would mean increased capabilities. So how can man increase his mental capacity? What about the other 95% of the brain, and what about the spiritual side of man? Can these give us higher intelligence?

The brain as we know it seems to be based on the five senses and the ability to think and visualize. Simple experiments show that it is not a source of overwhelming intelligence. It is a mechanical process and is a product of your genetic heritage, your memory, and your ability to talk to yourself. We must look elsewhere for a source of real intelligence and power.

Within our bodies lies our greatest treasure. It is like a doorway to our true home, yet no one can see it and it cannot be found. It is the source of our consciousness. It is a body of power and light. Without its light, we would not be conscious. Without its power, we would not have life. This power is the spark that animates and illuminates the mechanical body and mind. The body and mind have no life of their own. It is the body of light and power which has what we think of as life. It temporarily illuminates and gives power to this mechanical frame and leaves it at the time of death.

Your power body exists in a different realm than does your physical body. Your body of power and light exists in the second level of existence, and your physical body in the third. Your power is made up of an unusual form of energy or light, a part of the fabric of the universal power and light which is the essence of this physical universe. When this universal power and light divides and becomes differentiated into individual beings of light, your power is created. Your power exists in a realm whose very essence is power.

Within your power there is a superior consciousness. It is different than the brain's consciousness. It has a type of awareness or knowingness that is more profound. Our eyes cannot see through walls, but power doesn't have those limitations. It is not limited by the physical world, but it is intimately tied to your physical body, and as long as it is encased in that vessel its full power remains unconscious. It appears to have been trapped in a dream and has lost the memory of its true nature. This fragment of power that is your spark of life is the only way you can see through the limitations of the mind and the senses. It is the beginning of your spiritual quest to discover Power's full splendor.

Your power does not reside in the body, as your stomach does. Your power is not in the physical world, yet it does affect the physical world. A common example of this is the light from the sun. The sun's light is not physical, yet it brings life to everything on this planet. Your power is the same. It can change and affect the material world, just as sunlight can.

Your power body

Your power is an unusual formation of light that appears as a somewhat oblong ball of light, which is generally felt and experienced in the heart or stomach area. This is the seat of your power, your higher intelligence. From this center your light functions at your unconscious command to illuminate and give consciousness to the physical mechanism.

When you want to think, you unconsciously send a ray or beam of your light and power to your head and feel yourself located there. You immediately identify with what your power illuminates, in this case thoughts, and you feel that you are the mind and thoughts. When you feel your hand you send a ray of your power to that area, so that it becomes illuminated and then you feel.

You may remember a time when you were cut and didn't feel any pain until you saw your injury. This is because the pain didn't become conscious until you directed your power and light there. You might say that the pain did not come to light. This also explains the amazing cases that have been documented of people having control over pain. If the light is not directed to the pain, it does not come to light and is not known about.

Your power and light can be directed in a similar fashion outside the physical body. While your power is generally inside the physical body, it is in no way trapped inside it. You may have had the experience of driving down the road and seeing someone in the car next to you. You think about them, and they immediately turn and look straight at you. Have you noticed that they seem to know exactly where you are? They don't look at anybody else. You may have had it happen in a crowded room, when the person looked straight at you and not at anybody else. What happened? You unconsciously sent a ray of your power and light over to that person and touched them, and their power felt the touch and responded. The person who was touched was as unconscious as you were about what happened. This is an every-day example of the unconscious use of your power.

You can experiment with sending your power outside your body. You can learn how to touch people and have them feel your power touch their body. You can feel objects far away from your body and can understand what they are made of and what their internal structure is. It is control and use of your power and light that will be the basis for everything that we do.

It is this power that can give you the higher intelligence that is not based on the mechanical brain or on its memory system. Your brain, the physical mechanism, has only the imagination and the senses, which are not real power and intelligence. These exist in a realm where there are no senses or mechanical brains; their under-standing is non-physical, yet they empower the body just as the sun nourishes all living things. Your power has a higher intelligence than the brain, but your power and your brain exist in two different worlds. How can your brain receive the higher intelligence of power when your brain knows only words, images, and feelings, and your power communicates with rays of a special light? The mechanical brain cannot understand the language of power. The knowledge of power is unconscious to the brain. The solution is to get the knowledge of your power translated into the mechanical brain, so that this knowledge can become a thought that you are conscious of.

First, you have to enter your power and do everything from there. You have to function from your power. Without being in your power and acting from there, you are just using your mind and your imagination, and there will be nothing from your power. Relaxing your body and slowing down the mind will help you find your power, because your power is not part of your body. It is beyond the body. Your power is the real you. When you enter your power, you're not doing anything special. You will enter your power when you stop doing anything special.

Relaxing the body can be done in any number of ways. Meditation techniques like yoga or Zen are fine. Hypnotic techniques will also work. Many times just sitting and taking several relaxing breaths are all you need. You may have your own technique for relaxation; you may want to just shut your eyes and imagine yourself someplace where you feel relaxed.

Whatever technique you use, relaxing your physical body will have a deep effect on the state of the brain. Your mind will immediately feel the effects of the relaxation. Fewer demands are put on your brain to respond and control. When your eyes are closed and your body is still, your brain will begin to calm.

Because there are no concrete physical guideposts, silencing your brain becomes an art form. Keeping your eyes closed and your body motionless will help, but there needs to be more. If your eyes are left unmoving and relaxed, something special happens to the brain. Every time the eyes move there is an automatic brain response.

You may be aware of the studies done on dreaming. When subjects are sound asleep, their eyes don't move. As soon as they begin to dream, a continuous, rapid eye movement begins to take place. The images and thoughts of the mind are connected to the movement of the eyes. If you want to calm your mind, don't move your eyes. You can experiment with this for yourself. Take a familiar object like a candle flame and stare at it. In a few seconds you will begin to notice that your thoughts seem to vanish and there are spaces in your consciousness lasting a second or two.

When your body and mind are still, a certain clarity begins to take place. It's a strange point. You can look into your deeper nature. You can look into what awareness is. When you see a tree, you know that there is a distance between your awareness and the tree. You know that the tree is over there and you are seeing it from here. When you think of a tree in your mind, your awareness perceives an image of a tree in your mind. The image of the tree is not you. It is an object of your awareness, just as the physical tree is an object of your awareness.

When you see something outside your mind, it is an object of your awareness, and when you see an image in your mind, it is still just an object of your awareness. The image is not you or your awareness. Yet, in our everyday lives we live as though we are the images in our minds. We do not sense that these images are just as much objects of our awareness as a tree is. We feel that we are this mind and body, yet they are objects of perception. They are not you or your awareness. It is simple to understand that if you see a tree, you are not going to think that you are the tree. Although you can see that your thoughts are objects of perception, we somehow become so identified with them that they seem as if they are us. Similarly, when someone close dies, we may feel as if a part of us dies, too. Our true self, our power, becomes identified with objects of perception.

We have become so accustomed to the sound of our voice in our minds that we feel frightened if we are not talking to ourselves. If you spoke your thoughts out loud, others would think you a crazy person. If you silently talk to yourself, no one knows and your craziness can go undetected. Our awareness has become so identified with the thoughts and images in our brain that we assume we are those thoughts and images, and we feel frightened if they are not there.

Overcoming fear and freeing your awareness from identification is precisely what is needed in order to enter your power and use your wisdom. Your thoughts are like the rear-view mirror in your car. As long as you are staring into your rear view mirror, you won't be able to drive. You have to give up the feeling that the rear view mirror (your mind), is the only thing happening in your life, so that you can get in touch with your higher intelligence.

When you have calmed the body and mind, and have seen with clarity that the mind is an object, you see that everything that is occurring is an object, and that the only thing that is not an object is your awareness. What is this awareness that cannot see itself? This awareness is your power body. It is the spark of life that empowers your being. It is a drop in the ocean of power and light. It is your share of the infinite.

Your awareness is the power and light that illumines your body and mind. When you direct this light, it illumines the object and there is awareness of the object. When your mind repeats the experience, you create your consciousness. Then your power feels identified with something that it illuminates. It becomes too narrow and contracted, and you feel that you are your body and mind. You have lost the feeling that you are the light, and instead of merely being aware of the body and mind, you feel that you are this body and mind. You have become identified with a mechanical process and now perceive only the darkness of mind and body. When you begin to perceive your power, you will become aware that it is your power that has the light of awareness. It is the light of your power that is illuminating your mind, and it is that illumination which is creating your awareness of your human consciousness.

This illumination will give you higher intelligence and the power to create the future. The light of your power has a remarkable quality. In our physical world, when the sun shines, darkness disappears. When you direct the light of your power to illumine your mind, the darkness in the mind tends to clear up. The more illumination directed into the mind, the more the mind tends to clarify.

There are hallucinations or shadows that come into the mind that are the product of its mechanical nature. They may be crazy ideas or strange visions, and for the mind that is not illuminated, they are taken to be real, and delusions result. For the mind that is illuminated by the light of power, these dark forms simply fade away. What does not fade away in the strong illumination of your power will be the truth.

Without the power of illumination the mind is just doing its mechanical job. It is creating a pond where the waters are muddied by thought. When your body and mind are stilled, and the mind is seen to be an object of perception, your light and power are discovered. You can direct your power and light toward the mind, and the mechanism of the mind will be cleansed from a higher source. The delusions of the mind will disappear and only higher intelligence will remain. You will have found the wisdom of your power.

THE BODY OF POWER

The ultimate technique of power returns you to the awareness of your original oneness with the universe. It imbues your being with the highest wisdom and power; you become an incarnation of Power. When you have arrived at this state, you are no longer searching for power and light. You have become power and light. This is the ultimate state of awareness, where the limited powers are no longer separate. They are one power, one being. That being is you—not the one that is trapped inside a human shell. This is the real you, radiant, liberated, boundless, the home of wisdom and power.

The techniques of power are available to you for your spiritual quest. The techniques are milestones along the way to the highest source. You can use your wisdom and power to overcome the obstacles of the lower worlds of fear and contraction. The heavy burdens and dark coverings of the lower forms of mentality make it difficult to advance quickly. Spiritual power can be used to speed the search for the highest awareness and intelligence within. Higher intelligence is spiritual power, and the use of spiritual power to find the truth and bring that truth into the world is the exercise of your spirituality.

All wisdom and power in the universe is part of the highest Power, and the discovery and use of spiritual power to promote the growth of spiritual and material blessings is a necessity.

There may be nothing in a person's past or present that would allow spiritual development. Everywhere fear is promoted to maintain worldly power, and people become frightened of anything spiritual, preferring something false. We must clear the blocks and use our spiritual power to break the deep seated habits of fear that destroy our progress. Spiritual progress has been limited because of this fear. It is an irrational fear that borders on insanity and has led people to destroy the light rather than face it.

Is it possible to change the world with power? For any worldwide change to take place, you need to have the power to break through your fear and contraction. The power to change the world and to create the future must be given away. Then and only then can you move quickly enough to make a change in the world.

This power is not the human body, the mind, or the imagination. It is a subtle, non-physical essence that must be discovered. You are not trying to make the physical world do something that it is not capable of doing. You are using the power that animates the material world. You are looking for the wisdom and power to create the future that your highest intelligence has directed you to create for yourself and for the world. Without this highest purpose everything that you do is useless. It is only through lack of wisdom that you continue to use your power to create the contracted and fearful state that is wasting your power and making you an impotent human being. You must seek the highest wisdom and power and create a future for yourself that will be without the contraction and fear that is the hallmark of human consciousness. Without this beginning, the light will be too bright and you will react with fear and be unable to continue.

Your power and light dwells at the center of your being. Whenever you give up your outward activities, you naturally draw back into your higher nature, back into the source of your higher intelligence. When you sleep at night, or when you relax, you may find yourself feeling weightless. You may feel a pleasant vibrating energy coursing through your body. When you find yourself very tired and you sit in a comfortable chair, your mental activity may stop and you will have a sinking feeling; you may feel an incredible peace and joy come to you. You may have seen an incredible sunset and been shocked at seeing such beauty. Your thoughts were silent for a moment and you noticed a peace and a beauty within you.

Occasionally we drop into a deeper state wherein we can taste something more. But it seems so useless in our society. We have been trained to think that we are the brain, and if we are not feverishly thinking, then something is wrong. It is when our mind is not regarded with such importance, when our body and mind are relaxed, that we can step into something more. When you are tired and you rest, you may feel that you are somehow more within your body. When you are thinking, you will notice that you feel like you are more in your head. When you are relaxed and drop from the head into the center of your being, you will feel this dropping sensation. When you are thinking, you will feel yourself—your center of focus—behind the eyes in the brain. The dropping sensation is your center of focus coming back down into the center of your being, down to where your power connects to the body, where you feel it connect; and that is near the heart or stomach area.

For a higher intelligence to come into your life and for your brain to stop being the source of your intelligence, you need to learn the art of living in the presence of power near the heart. Living as power instead of as the brain has unbelievable benefits. When you function from the brain, you are not in contact with the world. Your thoughts tell you that you are, but you are not. When you think about the world, you are actually only contacting the thought and the images that are in your brain. For instance, if you see someone you had an argument with yesterday, immediately the memory of that argument comes to your mind, and you react to the memory. You are doing what your memory of yesterday is telling you to do. You are not aware of what is occurring now, because you are only reacting to the images. You are getting angry as the person approaches, and suddenly you see that it is someone else. You feel embarrassed seeing your mistake and realizing what you are doing.

In contrast, when you are in your power, you see the memory flash through your brain. You are conscious of thoughts, but you understand them to be just another object of perception. You don't feel that the memory is you, so you don't obey it. You don't get trapped in a viewpoint just because your brain is working and a thought passed by. You continue to respond to actual events as they occur. Your natural state of universal love still flows forth. You don't get caught acting a certain way towards anyone. You are still just you, and you don't change. When you act from your power, you are responding to the world. You are having a relationship with people, not with your mind. You are involved with what is happening, not with what you are thinking.

When you are acting from the brain, you are setting up a distance between yourself and the world. Your thoughts create the feeling that you are here and they are there. When you relate to your friends through thought, your natural love disappears, and you create a distance. Your thinking is the result of a deep fear. You need the distance to exercise control. You cannot feel close to something and control it, so you become afraid and create a distance using your thought. You can't feel love for something you fear. When you act from the mind, you cannot know love.

Your brain is a machine that you use to generate images and the sound of speech. If you relate to the picture in your mind, you are not relating to the person. If you are not relating to the person, how can love exist? There is just your fear and your thoughts; you will naturally experience loneliness. You are cut off from your friends, and you are cut off from the world. You are living in a dream, and cannot relate to the world.

The process of love is a totally different phenomenon. It does not happen in your head. When you relate to the world from your mind, you feel that your center of focus is in your head. When you act from your power, you act from your love. You act from the center of your being and you un-

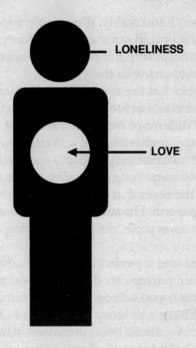

Your power is your love

derstand what love is. You have the ability to respond to the world as it is. You have a relationship with the world and the ability to love.

I once saw a concert on television with an orchestra and a violinist. As soon as I saw the violinist, I could see that he was acting from his power. I had never seen the violinist or the orchestra before, and had no particular interest in the music. Remarkably, it was only a videotape on TV, yet I could see that the musician was acting from his power. It is rare to see someone who has any contact with their power.

I looked at the rest of the orchestra, where everyone else was functioning from their heads, and the difference between the soloist and the rest of the orchestra was unbelievable. Every note the violinist played had a quality about it. There was something magical about the notes he played; the notes that others played were empty by comparison. His sounds were solid and substantial; everyone else was making hollow sounds.

Here was a perfect example of what acting from your power can do. When you act from your center, you will be doing real things. Your acts will have a potency that your mind cannot produce. A violinist became the best in the world because he had stumbled on a secret, and the secret was to act from his power and not from his brain. When you act from your brain, you are not doing anything real. It is like watching a movie of people riding in a roller coaster and believing that you are riding with them. In your brain you are living in a dream, and you can spend your life thinking you are doing things—but you will only be a technician. You will be going through the motions as if you were doing something, but your acts will be hollow, and they will have no potency in the world because you have no relationship with the world. Your relationship will be with the images in your mind.

A pleasant dream is pleasant entertainment, but spending your entire life in dreams is a form of insanity. You will have good dreams and laugh, and you will have bad dreams and cry. If you are not lost in dreams, you will see people laughing and crying, when nothing is happening to them except their dreams. You will know that happiness is not being caught in the crazy web of dreams, in the constant grinding of thought. Happinesss is moving back to the source, back to the fountain of life—your power at the center of your being. There you will find your truth, meaning, and purpose. You will find the power to fulfill your life. Then you will have the happiness of the spiritual world as well as the happiness of the material world.

WISDOM OF
THE POWER BODY

What is intelligence? Some people might say that it is a measurement of various mental skills. Some might say that it is the higher mental functioning of thought. Some might mention the evolution of the species and say that it was the development of the cerebral cortex in man's brain that gave him intelligence. From whatever source, all of the current definitions of intelligence are based on the mechanical nature of the brain.

Science tells us that if we add certain chemicals to our diet or stimulate the brain, we can increase intelligence. Yet science is also aware that only a small portion of the brain is being used at any one time. Science speculates that there may have been some sort of trauma that has caused the limitation in the brain and that we could be more intelligent if we used more of our brain.

But what is intelligence? Don't we believe that thought is the source of intelligence? If we can't think, we are an idiot, retarded. Something must be wrong with us, but what is thought? When you watch your thoughts, you witness your brain recreating the sound of words, and you realize that you are just talking to yourself. Your ability to think is your ability to talk to yourself, and the ability to talk to yourself is not a measure of great intelligence.

A small intelligence does appear when you use language. There is a certain solidification of ideas when words are used to explain a concept. The more you speak about something, the more your ideas come together to paint a complete picture. When your words have painted a complete picture, you feel you have understood something. You have understood through words. This is thought to be intelligence.

The highest intelligence doesn't involve the brain at all. It is the intelligence of your inner power. It is the intelligence of the universal power and light. When you translate the intelligence of power into the human mind, it becomes the highest intelligence your mind is capable of. It is not based on the memory of the past and is not a product of language and thought. It is based on the principle that there is a universal power behind this world, and that you have a share in it. You have the ability to understand universal wisdom.

The easiest way for you to use your higher intelligence and begin your spiritual quest is to understand the wisdom of the power body. The power body is a ball of light and power that is your spark of life. It is a fragment of the universal power and light and possesses a fragment of its wisdom.

Your power has a natural intelligence. It has the natural ability to see through and eliminate things that are not in harmony with it. It is like the sun shining on the world. When the morning comes and the sun rises in the sky, the chill and the darkness of the world disappear. When you enter your power, the chill and darkness of the world disappear from your life. Your power is the source of your love, and it brings warmth to your life.

The wisdom of the power body is just the wisdom of being able to see through the illusions of the physical world. Your power is the light of higher intelligence, and the darkness of ignorance is the brain and the world. Your brain is a mechanical device that has no life or consciousness. Its chemical and electrical processes create your thought, your memory, and the senses. The light of your power sees the brain as an object of perception, and it sees a coarse, contracted energy. You can purposefully illuminate the brain with the light of your power and destroy the dark illusions that it creates. This is the natural wisdom of your power.

Most of the time, the information running through our brains is just the brain making noise. For the information to be of a different quality, and to partake of a higher truth, the mental processes have to be illuminated by the light of the power body in a very directed way. If the light of your power is not directed strongly, the information will remain the ramblings of memory and thought. The mind will not have the truth and validity that is found when it is directed by higher intelligence.

A mind that is directed by higher intelligence will be illumined and directed by the light of the power body. When the illumination of your power directs the brain, your brain will possess the wisdom that is beyond the brain's limitations. Without the brain being directed by the light of your power, there is just the mad mind continually churning through memories and words and not really saying anything true.

The truth enters consciousness because your light destroys the confusion of the mind. Only the truth remains in the light of your power. Everything that is not true turns into a shadow in the mind and disappears. When you can function from the center of your being, when you can illumine the mind with light, then you will be emptying the mind of the false. Real intelligence is not having false things in the mind. Real intelligence is knowing the truth of things, not being deluded by your fears, thoughts or memories.

In order to find the mysterious source of the light that dispels the delusions of the mind, you must be able to calm the body and mind to the point where they are no longer a distraction. Your power is not a physical phenomenon. If you keep the physical disturbances at a minimum while you are just beginning, it will be of great help. Later, when you are more familiar with the presence of your power, you won't need any preparation. You will be within your power during your everyday activities.

In the beginning, however, you will find it very useful to develop a system of relaxation, so that you can begin to use your power regularly. Any technique for relaxation that you are familiar with makes a good beginning. You may just want to start by taking several deep, relaxing breaths and feeling the relaxation spread throughout your body as you exhale. After several breaths, begin at the top of your head and feel every part of your body deeply relax. When your body is relaxed, you will find your mind has also become more quiet. When your mind is quiet, subtle experiences can be perceived. You will become more sensitive and perceptive.

As long as your mind is thinking and churning, you will not be able to experience your power. It will be functioning and you will even be using it, but you won't have any control. You will not be using your power in such a way that your mind will be imbued with truth. We are habitually thinking about everything that is going on around us, and we are blocking our higher intelligence. We need a technique to quickly and easily bypass our thoughts so that we can use our power.

Here is the problem. We are lonely, so we talk to ourselves. We love to listen to the sound of our own voice, so we use our brain to hold discussions with ourselves. We get frightened when anything else happens, and yet the brain doesn't have much to say. Previously, we spoke of fear and contraction as being the only problem, and that fear shows itself as an inability to listen to anything but your own thoughts. The ability to listen requires that the mind be quiet so that new information can enter. If the mind is filled with the noise of your thoughts, then no new information can come in. We use the noise level as a fearful response to keep new information out so we won't be threatened. You are using the noise level in your head to keep the unconscious mind in existence. Fear is the enemy and the noise of the brain is its weapon.

A valuable technique, then, is to notice your hearing. Don't try and listen to anything; you will just be creating more noise if you do that. You want to very quietly, very patiently, just notice the hearing. You don't want to pay attention to any sounds, because you will be repeating that noise in the brain in order to hear it. The act of noticing is a very quiet act. It is not thinking about something. It is an act of attention, directing your attention toward your hearing—not the sounds, just the hearing.

The hearing is a very quiet phenomenon. Noticing the hearing will suddenly disconnect the illumination of your power from the mind and connect it to something which is familiar, not threatening, and very capable of taking you quickly away from your preoccupation with your brain and its noise. As you continue to carefully notice your hearing, you will find a peace beginning to come to your body and mind. It will seem like the whole world is quieter, even though there may be noise in your environment.

When you get the feeling that the world is somehow quieter, it is your brain becoming quieter, and it is an excellent confirmation that you are doing things well. It is an excellent exercise for your everyday life to be able to practice and experience this peace and quiet in your mind as much as possible.

When you begin to experience the quiet of the world, begin to notice softer and softer sounds. When you find one soft sound, look for the next softer sound, and so on till you have found several sounds, each one softer than the last. Then notice the softest sound you can find. Take a minute and notice the softest sound. When you have found the softest sound, see if you have noticed the sound of your breath. Look closely to see if your breath is the softest sound. See if you have noticed your heartbeat. Is your heartbeat the softest sound? Can you then hear the silence behind everything?

When you have gone this far, you will notice several changes. The senses will have changed in a very unique way. When you are in your power, your hearing will not feel like normal hearing; it will be more like feeling. If you shut your eyes, you will see that your hearing is now somewhat like feeling. Your hearing will have changed, and it will have become a mixture of feeling and hearing. If your hearing has changed like this, it is an excellent indication that you have entered into your power, and you have entered well enough to begin using it consciously.

The body of power inside of you does not have seeing and hearing the way your body does. Its power is not based on anything physical. Your power does not have human senses at all. It has only one power, and all the powers we call senses are merged into one sensory power. Your power can have all the senses. When your hearing becomes like feeling, you have entered into your power and are experiencing the senses of your power, not the senses of your body.

Your power is just power and light, and the division into seeing, hearing and feeling is made strictly because of the human mind. So, when you are using the techniques of power, you will be able to understand how to feel with your eyes and see with your ears, and you will become accustomed to the change in your hearing as one of the first symptoms of being at the threshold of your power.

There are other ways of telling if you have entered into your power. There are other symptoms. Your center of focus should have shifted. Your center of focus is that feeling of "I", where you are centered in your body. Normally, when you do anything, your center of focus is in your head. This is because we have identified ourselves with our brain, and we feel we are our heads. When you enter your power body, your center of focus will be at your power, and you will feel that you have dropped down around the stomach or chest area, somewhere near the heart. You will have the definite feeling that you are not looking with your eyes, but that your vision starts down inside your body, at your power. Your power is not associated with the heart and is not associated with the emotional feelings people feel there. Your power is not a physical phenomenon. It associates with your physical body, but it is simply your share of the universal power and light.

Your power is a rather large oblong ball of unusual light located near the stomach or heart area. You may feel it even lower. It is not firmly connected to your body, and it's not really inside your body. It exists in a different realm. The location that you feel comes from your mental point of view. The brain still functions when you enter your power, and it experiences your power inside your body, around the stomach or heart area. Sometimes when you are tired and sit down to rest comfortably, you feel yourself automatically drop your thoughts, and you feel yourself sink into your body. This is a very important feeling to notice. You are dropping your preoccupation with your thoughts, and you are moving towards the center of your being, towards your power and light.

Whenever you enter your power at the center of your being, another feeling to be aware of is a change in consciousness. You will not have the strong feeling of "I" and "the world." That feeling will be gone, and you will feel a connection with your environment, a oneness. Power is not separate from the world. And only your power can experience your deepest love, which is not just an emotional state rooted in fear. This is the type of love that is felt when you experience your higher spiritual nature and understand that you are the world.

The first stage of the wisdom of the power body is just reawakening to the true love that is inside of you, the highest love. This love has the ability to totally transform your life. It can release you from the fear, loneliness, and separation of living as the thinking mind. The wisdom of knowing that you are not separate from people will totally transform your relationships with them. You will have real love, and your needy relationships based on fear will transform into real love. This will be the beginning of your taste of the wisdom of power.

The wisdom of power has more specific uses. Not only does it have the ability to transform your relationship with the world, but it can be used to solve the everyday problems of our lives. We can use our power to give us the truth about what is really happening, beyond the illusions of the senses, to us and to others. For instance, you want to know something about someone—your power can tell you what the truth is about them. You can find out whether they will do something or have done something. You can find out about yourself. What are your best qualities? What would be the results of a certain decision? What will happen in the future? A thousand questions can be accurately answered.

To use the wisdom of the power body, you must first enter your power and feel your presence at the heart. You must take care that your center of focus stays at that center, at your power. All the symptoms of being in your power should be present. The next step is to form an image of what you want to know about in your mind. Say, for instance, that you want to find out about somebody's health. Staying centered in your power at the heart, you would form an image of that person in your mind. The image of that person does not have to be exact or very clear.

Then you must very gently allow the light from your center to go up and out toward the image that you have in your mind. Touch the image with your light and power. Feel the image and illuminate it with the light from your heart. Stay centered in your power at the heart, and you will feel things about the image. Ideas about

The ray of power illuminating a mental image

what is going on with that person will come into your mind. If you are concerned about a person's health, imagine their entire body, and with the light from your power illumine the image of their body. The image will tell you where in their body there is a problem.

Use your power to scan the individual areas of the body. Very often the image will be dark where there is an illness. Don't force anything. Your own power and light will give you the truth in their own way. Just continue illumining and feeling the image, and watch your feelings and thoughts. Suddenly you will recognize that you know something about the image. For instance, while you are scanning the back with your light, perhaps you suddenly feel that their back hurts. It is a very subtle technique. The truth will always be very subtle in your mind. The technique is remarkably accurate, and almost anyone can do it with almost 100% accuracy.

One of the symptoms of being successful at this is that there is a distinct feeling of distance between you, in your power at the heart, and the image in the mind. The distance seems farther than would any physical space. This is a key point. There is the chance that you have created the entire adventure in your mind, and in that instance you will notice a distinct difference between the two experiences. When you are just dreaming the whole experience, you will find it very difficult to get the distance, and the process of reaching up and out with your power won't feel right; the image will be too close. If you look at what is happening, you will find that your center is in the brain. Your ability to illuminate the mind will not feel right, and you won't find any light. When you illumine well, the image should get very sharp and clear. The sharper and clearer the image, the more illumination you have generated.

This technique of power is a very useful tool. With this tool you can gain very accurate knowledge about almost anything. If you are faced with a decision about a person, and you need to know about them, you can look into them, and everything can be revealed. There are no secrets to the wisdom of your power body. That may be one of its dangers. You can know things that may not be for your own good, and you may just violate someone else's privacy. It is a very good tool for social and business decisions.

If you are involved with a decision, you can thoroughly investigate it, and even look into the hidden parts of the decision, parts that you couldn't know about except through your power. You can look into the people involved in a business decision. You can tell whether a person is being honest with you or not, or whether there are hidden parts of an agreement that will not be beneficial to you. You can look into a business and see if it will be profitable. Using your power will give you the intelligence you need to conduct your life very clearly and successfully.

Using the wisdom of your power is not a spiritual tool in itself. It is an introduction to the power and light of your spiritual essence, and it can be used to discover things that will help you on your spiritual path. It is not spiritual because your mind still retains control, and the technique does not liberate you from the grip of fear and contraction that is keeping your mind in its limited state. It is a good beginning and can deeply affect your life, but it is just the first step on the greater road to perfection.

THE HEALING VIBRATION

*H*ealing is a magnificent science, a dream of mankind. How is it done?

We have all heard the stories. Some of us have even done healing. Others have been healed. But for the vast majority of mankind, there has been no real direct experience. We are going to change that.

Previously, healers were so rare that for a variety of reasons they did not come forth to reveal themselves. The techniques that they used were hidden as well. Now this, too, is changing. Initially we will discuss some background information, so that we will all be communicating on the same level.

The universe and everything we know is made up of vibrations. Scientists are now admitting this simple fact. What it means is that whoever can control vibrations can control the world.

It sounds simple, but look down through history and note how many people controlled the world—not many. And those who did were not very helpful in bringing this knowledge to the masses. This is going to change. What we are going to discuss is how you and I can learn to control the vibrations of the world and begin the healing process.

Healing is a vast subject. Most people think that when you have an illness, you need healing. This is the most obvious form of healing, but it is only the first step. The road is very long. The perfect healer is the perfected man. You don't become a great healer without becoming a great being. As you progress in your healing, you will also be progressing in your spiritual growth and power.

Your spiritual growth is the most important aspect of healing ability. In the final analysis, when you are healing your physical body, you are also permeating yourself with spiritual vibrations, and the healing that takes place is your body manifesting the vibrations of spiritual levels in which there is no such thing as disease and disharmony. There is a natural vibration for your perfected form which during illness is lost for a time or is disturbed, leading to the breakdown of your physical form.

First, you must have great patience, because you are going to be changing the physical body. We would all prefer instant cures with angels singing and great bursts of light, but that may not be possible. Our method is easier. The changes you make will happen at the subatomic level, so a little patience will be required.

The second thing that is required is love. You will need love because it is the strongest healing vibration that you are familiar with. Love can take you far, and can sometimes bring about the healing process. We want healing with control, so love will be helpful; but it will not be the real key.

To begin the real process you need to know how to still the mind in a very special way. You may have noticed how many relaxation or meditation techniques make you drowsy or put you to sleep. We are aiming instead at a very special state called "entering your power;" in which your senses expand, change, and become extrasensory. Here the senses of the physical body are expanded by the awareness of the power near the heart and become capable of knowing things. It is with the power and light at the heart that we begin the true healing work.

Here's how it's done. You begin by entering into your power at the heart, and then in your mind you form an image of something like the numbers on your radio dial. In this case it will be the range of vibrations or sounds from the highest to the lowest. You might put the low notes on the left side of the scale and the high notes on the right side.

HEALING

LOW
NOTES |—————————————————————| HIGH
NOTES

Vibrational Diagram

From your power at the heart you want to
direct a beam or a ray of your power, reaching out
with this power as if it were feeling and illuminating the sounds on the dial. The first thing that you
want to feel is the solidity of the image that you
have in your mind. Your power touches it, and
there seems to be some substance to it. When
your power illumines it, it does not feel like a
mirage.

Next you want to start at one end of the dial
and scan the range of vibrations, or sounds, and
find the vibration you are looking for. Say you
have a headache. First you enter your power at
the heart, then you create the image of your vibrational diagram in your mind. Each person
may have his own diagram or picture. You are
looking for the vibration that will cure the headache. You reach out with your light and power
and feel the sounds or vibrations as you begin

scanning. Sometimes the image itself will indicate the vibration we are looking for. There may occur a mark at the point where your special vibration occurs. Your power has the wisdom to know where it is and its illumination and power may indicate the vibration very quickly. Most often you will need to use your power to search for the vibration.

How you actually search for the vibration is not particularly important. What *is* very important is recognizing when you have found the location and the vibration. When you are scanning and feeling the sounds or vibrations with your power, there will be a jolt in your power. It may also happen that the position of the vibration will mark itself in the image, and there will be a jolt in your power. The jolt or reaction of your power is the first key. Immediately after you feel the jolt in the power, the seat of your power near the heart will have a reaction. There is an automatic response which will feel like the emotion of love. It will not be an emotion, it will be the sudden sensing of the healing vibration.

This is a very critical and difficult moment. You have found the vibration. Your power must stay concentrated on and feel the exact vibration. You are actually dividing your attention between feeling the vibration and watching the heart area to make sure that the vibration is creating the healing feeling, which is something like the emotion of love, at the heart.

HEALING

When you feel that you have contacted the correct sound or vibration, you want the power itself to begin vibrating at the same frequency. If you feel the vibration as a sound, your power should begin making the same sound. Your power continues to stay concentrated on the image, feeling the sound or vibration, and noticing the healing feeling at the heart. Then you begin to imitate, take in and imbibe the vibration or sound into your power. Your power matches and becomes the vibration. It resonates at the same frequency. This may take a little practice but it is not too difficult.

Within a few seconds you should begin to notice a vibrational change in the entire body. You will feel more alert, more awake, more whole. You will feel a sudden goodness throughout the body. What is happening is that the vibration is having an effect on your entire body. There are disharmonious energies throughout our bodies. They become a chaos of different frequencies. When the power takes one sound and resonates with that one frequency, all the disharmonious energies vanish and you are left feeling immediately clean. When the light of your power radiates through and illumines the physical body and mind, those things that are not compatible with that higher truth disappear, and you become conscious of higher truth.

The feeling of being cleansed is a good confirmation that you are doing things well and that

HEALING

you have received an immediate benefit. Now you must increase the strength of the vibration in your power. Not only should the power begin to feel stronger, but the sound should increase in strength. It should feel like the center of your being growing stronger. When your power is firmly resonating as the healing vibration, allow your power to begin to expand and fill the entire physical body as the strength and power of the sound continues to grow.

Allow the power to expand just a short space outside the body, and continue to feel the strength of the sound. Now allow the power to go far outside the body, expanding into the universe, with the sound continuing to gather strength. Continue expanding this power farther and farther out into the universe, while you continue to maintain the same vibration and sound. After a few minutes you can return the power back to the center of your being and return to your waking state. You will find yourself in a very heightened state of health and alertness. If you want to feel this way again at another time, practice resonating your power at that frequency either while you are quiet or during your activities. As you grow in the technique your healing abilities will naturally get better and better, and you will be able to heal yourself and others.

THE EMANATION AND EMBODIMENT OF POWER

*O*ur conscious mind is very limited. Science tells us that we use only about 5% of our brain, and this small part of our mind that is conscious has only one method of understanding the world. The method of the mind is the thinking process, and everything that man has created is the product of thought.

The thinking mind that has created the world has a unique intelligence. It enables us to survive; and thought has allowed the human species to dominate all the other animals of the world. It has been our greatest survival technique. We have learned to think, to control, and to dominate—because of fear. Fear has brought on the modern world, but there is more to intelligent life than our fear and our need to survive through words and images.

We have the ability to analyze and dissect

and understand through words, but the thinking mind is trapped by the words and images it creates. Those words and images are not real. They are used to analyze the past in order to survive and to create a better future. When words are all you know, every action will be based on fear and will be an attempt to control and dominate. You will be unable to love and to relate directly with the world around you. Your relationship will be with the words and images in your brain. You will not be responding to the world. You will have no relationship with it. You will feel separate and alone. You will be trapped in the prison of fear.

There is another way to live, and a totally different way of relating. This other way is through love. Your love is not a thought or an image in the brain, nor is your love an emotional reaction to a thought or image in the brain. A love such as that is no relationship at all. It is just you, relating to something in your mind. It has no reality outside your mind. It is your attempt to dominate and control your environment, and to get what you want. It is your mind having a self-centered dream. Love is not found in the brain. Love is not some chemical or electrical brain phenomenon. How could love be so cheap and narrow? Love is something totally different.

Love is the experience of your higher intelligence, the power and light that are your innermost core. The natural understanding and functioning of your power is love. When you are functioning from your power, you have the capacity to love. You have the capacity to give love and receive love. If you are functioning from the brain, you only have the capacity for survival. Living your life from your power is very holistic and very healing, and it has almost been forgotten in our modern world. We have learned to survive, but we haven't learned about love and spiritual intelligence. Love will enter your life only by an understanding of the deeper levels of power.

In order to understand the deeper levels, the spiritual levels, your power must contact higher spiritual sources. You are stuck in your physical experiences, and this preoccupation with the physical body and mind has caused you to lose the vision of the higher realm of power and light. Your power dwells in this higher realm, but your consciousness does not. You remain unconscious of the wisdom of your power.

It is very helpful to find mentors—spiritual powers with great intelligence. If you want spiritual advancement, you must find those who have it and listen to them. They are available to you. There are great spiritual emanations of the supreme Power who appear in the universal power and light who can be contacted by your power. Your power has the potential of understanding the state of power and has the opportunity to commune with an emanation of the highest Power. You can bring that power and light into the world, and you can begin the transformation of this physical existence.

The world of power is the world of love, and the emanations of power that appear there are the embodiments of love. Your physical body and mind cannot understand love. The brain is a survival mechanism, and it is always afraid. The realm of power is the only place where love exists, and these emanations of Power are emanations of love. They are not trapped in the fear and survival of the world.

You should become aware of these great embodiments of love that exist in the universal power and light that are available to guide you in your spiritual growth. These beings love you more than you can comprehend. In all your experiences, you have only been listening to your mind, and your mind has no love. What you have there are the replicas of love. The highest spiritual powers are available to show you what love is, and they will change your life. They are the greatest friends that you can have. Befriend them and take their advice; listen to them carefully and do what they say. They will be your highest and best spiritual advisors, and they will show you the quickest way to taste the ecstasy of higher spiritual consciousness. You will finally have a taste of love, the most fulfilling experience of your life.

On the next page is a diagram of human consciousness. It is a diagram of how you will be meeting and communicating with the emanations of Power. The mind has two paths by which it can receive information. One is the path of thought, and the other is the path of power. Our normal way of understanding the world is through the mechanism of thought. We create the feeling of the world by thinking about something, and then it becomes conscious. When you think about things, your world is divided into you and the world, and there is no communion. There is another path which unifies both the inward and the outward. It is the path of love, and it needs some discussion, as this is the path that we are going to be taking in our spiritual journey. The path of love is the path of your power. Your power feels communion with the world. It feels love and can communicate with the world, and it is not alone.

We should understand the two ways we receive information, because although we know the intelligence of the brain and its words, it is the path of love that is the path of higher intelligence. The path of fear, the thought process, is the path of limited intelligence. As you learn the techniques of power, you will need to be able to determine which path you are taking. All the techniques of power are based on the path of love and will only work when you are in your power. This one fact of being able to tell whether

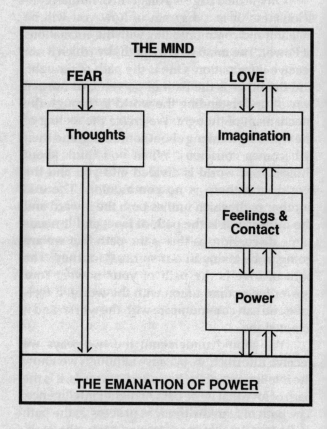

you are in a state of fear-based thought with limited intelligence or whether you are in a loving, unified state of higher intelligence will alter your life more than any other knowledge you may have gathered.

For you to perfect the power techniques, you must be able to tell whether you are in your mind or in your power. When you are in your mind, your center of focus and your awareness are in your mind. When you are in your power, your center of focus will be near the heart or stomach area. When you are in your mind, none of the techniques of power will work, and when you are in your power, everything will work.

Our normal conscious state is made up mostly of thought. You need to open the deeper levels of your being to your awareness. There is a subconscious mind and an unconscious mind. The subconscious mind is the part of your mind where you hold the truth that you deny. You need to listen, to have some silence and care, and make the truth available to yourself. This is a first step.

After you have opened the deeper levels of your being, you will be able to contact the world. You will be able to interact with it, and understand it. When you are thinking about the world, you don't make contact with it at all. You are watching and listening to your mind, and you distort everything to fit the way you think. If you are lost in your thoughts, you will feel lonely and cut off from the world. Nobody exists for you but yourself. On the spiritual path you will make contact, and you will end the feeling of being cut off. The loneliness and isolation that you feel will be healed.

In order to make conscious contact with spiritual intelligences, you will need to mechanically send a beam or a ray of your power and light to make contact with them. Spiritual contact is made in a very specific way. In the diagram on page 100, the contact is designated as two columns of arrows. It is actually an extension of your power and light. The arrows represent the two-way communication that occurs in the light.

You should get a very solid understanding of exactly how the ray of power is created and what you can expect. The ray you will be creating is the transmission of power from your power body to an emanation of power. Entities in the realm of power use this as their method of communication. The ray is a verifiable presence and is either an extension of your own power or the power body of a spiritual entity. Either way, it functions as a channel for communication between your power and a spiritual emanation.

When you are in your power and you use the ray of power to contact any object outside your body, your power creates a ray of light that makes contact with the object. It does so at your unconscious command as long as you are in your power. You must be able to translate the wisdom of your power for your conscious mind in order to know if your ray of power has made contact. After it has made contact, you can use the ray of power to send information about the object back to your conscious mind.

To create the ray of power and communicate with an emanation of Power, you must enter your power body by opening up the subconscious mind. You need to extend a cord-like ray of your power out and touch the entity that you wish to communicate with. Previously, when first learning to use the ray of power, you created an image in your mind that you illuminated. This process is radically different. You use your ray of power to discover what is already out there. From your power you probe around until you can feel and know you are contacting the emanation. When you are in your power, the emanation usually will already be contacting your power. This contact can be felt by the skin, which makes the emanation easier to find.

If you advance far enough, you will be able to see power extend out and touch things, and you will also be able to see power bodies and the emanations of Power. It is very real, and many people not only see the rays of power but hear their vibration. The light and power make a sound when sent as a ray. We all seem to be unconsciously using our power to communicate in this fashion, but we don't know how to control it. (For instance, the common situation in which you are

driving in your car and look over at someone,
and that person immediately turns and looks
directly at you as if they knew you were looking
at them. What you did was to unconsciously send
them a beam of your light, a beam of your power;
they were in a receptive mood and were unconsciously moved to look at who touched them.)

As soon as you contact any external object
with your power body, there is an immediate response. You can feel it. This is not the same as
normal feeling. You don't feel it with your body.
It seems as if the feeling is happening at the
object your power is touching, outside your body.
It is a feeling external to your body. The feelings
are occurring within the ray of power. You have
extended the ray of power outside your body,
and it feels as if you are touching something.
Your body is not touching anything, but it will
also react. These external feelings are the beginning of the process of translation that you must
carry out in order to understand the wisdom of
power. The ray of power and the transmission of
the information from the object is totally unconscious, but something is transmitted to the
feelings.

The first level of translation of the unconscious knowledge of power will be in the feelings.
The feelings themselves are for the most part
subconscious. Being in a heightened state of
awareness opens up the subconscious, so that
these feelings can be made conscious. They will

be the most accurate way for your physical being to begin to learn how to translate higher spiritual intelligence. The most accurate method is to not translate at all, but to just use your power to hear the spiritual entity communicate to you in language. Be aware that the feelings we are talking about are not associated with emotions. Emotions are very coarse and destructive to intelligence. Feelings are very subtle and delicate, even though there may sometimes be overwhelming, powerful feelings of love when you are with an emanation of Power. The feelings that you feel while translating seem undecipherable at first, because they are deeply subconscious. It takes continued use of the light of your power to decipher the feelings. Slowly at first, the light of your power will bring about more feelings and more clarity, and suddenly the next level of translation will occur: the imagination.

The imagination looks at the feelings and at first cannot translate such compact complexity. A continued quiet contact will provide more feeling, and then suddenly the imagination will understand the feelings or give an image that represents the feelings. The image occurs usually when you cannot or don't want to understand the message given by the feelings. The image is a translation of the feelings, and it can be used to further clarify the information coming to you in the ray of power. The image is felt to be outside the physical body.

The thinking mind is the next level of translation. Your mind becomes conscious of the images and feelings and translates them into words. The knowledge can then be written down and conveyed to others in this form, but the translation of the meaning into words almost destroys the message. It is said that a picture is worth a thousand words. The information coming through the ray of power is worth even more and is of such different quality that it takes a bit of patience and practice to really do any translation at all. With any translation much information is lost, and not all of the information is conveyed. The solidification of the knowledge transmitted from a higher level of consciousness into words at our level of consciousness is very difficult. A great multi-dimensional complexity ends up being translated and narrowed down into the meaning of words. How many words can be spoken about a leaf, and have you said them all?

When we seek spiritual help, we should contact the emanations of the highest spiritual Power. The emanations of that Power will have the highest wisdom and the greatest ability to help us fulfill our spiritual and material goals. They will help us create the future so that our highest purpose is quickly fulfilled.

The ultimate Power in the universe will be creating for your spiritual growth an emanation and embodiment of itself, which will be your spiritual friend and your doorway to spiritual wisdom and power. As you progress in your skills, you will learn how to experience the bliss of a high spiritual being. This bliss will change your life and enable you to rapidly develop spiritual qualities. You will be speaking with and learning from these beings, and their vibrations will begin to transform your lower vibrations. You will see through their eyes.

Because these embodiments or emanations of the one Power come from one source, they are one spiritual family, the family of Power. Your dedication to following truth and intelligence will enable you to join this spiritual family. They are the family of people who will be bringing the light into the world. They will be communing with the highest power and becoming the family of Power, incarnations of Power. They will become spiritually fulfilled.

The family of Power will be the creators of the future of mankind. Power gives them their highest purpose, and that wisdom guides them. They are given the power to create the future, and their highest purpose will be fulfilled. As they are fulfilled, humanity will be fulfilled.

Every person has something unique about them, something that they can be the most successful at, that will fulfill them. This purpose needs to be discovered and created. The highest power has a purpose for you, and that same power will help you create it. The members of this spiritual family find their highest purpose from the One Power, and together they fulfill their spiritual and material future.

To succeed in your spiritual and material quest, you need to have accurate communications with your emanation of Power. The translation process is very difficult and requires some care; and the main reason you may not be getting accurate information is that you don't want to receive it.

Changing and becoming more spiritual may be the last thing that you want. Most people think that if they talk about or listen to spiritual matters, they are being spiritual. They want to make it an emotional extravaganza or an inspirational event. Contacting and listening to spiritual intelligence is frightening. It is a shock. It is real, and it is a threat to your ego and your limited mind. It means change and seeing clearly, and unless you want to grow, you will block yourself from listening to higher intelligence. This means that you will subconsciously not communicate and pretend that you tried, or you will subconsciously and purposely mistranslate.

This can be seen when people are involved with a question of personal emotional involvement, for which they want to have an answer that is not true. Suddenly, they either get no information, or they don't translate what they do get, or they immediately forget that they got anything. Problems happen when your spiritual intelligence runs into your personal secret motives, your lower-life purpose. Your natural tendency is to get frightened and shrink away from the light, to preserve your secret motives. Your lower life purpose is what you are doing that is causing all the misery in your life. It is the reason things aren't going right. You think you are doing one thing, but secretly you are doing something totally different. To solve this problem you need to find your highest purpose and do it. The secret motives of your lower purpose will immediately cause the failure of both your highest intelligence and your highest purpose, and will eventually cause the failure of your life.

To translate higher intelligence, you will have to be honest with yourself. No one is perfect, and if you want spiritual growth, you have to admit to yourself that you may have to change. You must have the desire to change, not just the desire to talk about wanting to change. If you are not open to anything new or are just looking for entertainment, this level of spiritual skill will be unavailable to you. You will make it unavailable to yourself, and its availability is a reliable indicator as to your motives. When fear steps in and your mind shrinks from the light, you know you have reached an important point in your growth. Your growth only happens when you get past this point and listen with love and acceptance.

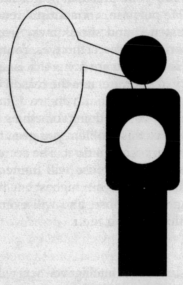

Communicating with an emanation of Power

Sometimes people communicate well for a time, and they get the same message over and over again about their lives. They think they want to change, but they are frightened. They give in to fear, and before long they can no longer get spiritual communication. It is not that they cannot communicate. They have stopped listening because they don't want to change. Growth is what matters. If you listen, you can grow. If you trust higher intelligence, understand what is being said to you, and allow it to change your life, you will be on track. Treat the presence of Power like a wise and loving friend that has your best interests at heart. Develop this relationship of trust, and your communication will grow and your life will be fulfilled. Here is a picture (page 110) of what will actually be happening when you communicate with one of the emanations of the highest power.

The power body, whether it is theirs or yours, tends to be an oblong, ball-like concentration of power. From your brain's perspective your power is felt to be inside your body near the heart or stomach area. From the perspective of power you are weightless and exist in a non-physical space, and you maintain a central presence inside the body but not of it. The emanations of Power will draw near you, often near your shoulder and head area. The size of their power body will be fairly large.

The emanation of power will initiate the communication by taking a beam or ray of its power and sending it down to connect to your power. You will be able to feel their presence, and you will be able to feel the touch of their power on your face or head, or wherever they send their ray of power through your body to reach your power. The ray of power they send to you is the beginning of the channel in which you will communicate. With a ray of your power, trace their beam of power back to them. You will be using your power to touch their power and you will both be participating in the channel of communication.

Your power does not have sense organs as your body does, so in order for you to understand anything consciously, your power will have to translate its knowledge for you. It's as if the wisdom of your power were a rainstorm, and you were standing under a tree to stay dry. The knowledge would be all around you, but after sifting through the leaves and branches of your brain, only a few drops would finally fall on your head. When you extend your power out to make contact, you don't pay attention to your mind, your thoughts, or the senses. Your power will be outside your body, and your translation is done at the end of the channel, at the emanation of Power. Your faculties for translation include your feeling, imagination, and thought. These faculties will be the raindrops that fall on your head. When your power knows something, your power causes the feelings to synchronize and resonate with the knowledge of power. Then the imagination and thought catch the spreading influence and your consciousness becomes imbued with wisdom. You must do the technique very carefully to avoid your mind's psychological filtering and denial. The symptoms of success will have all information occurring outside the body at the end of the ray of power.

The most accurate form of communication with your spiritual emanation will be to hear them speak to you in your language outside of your head. This is accomplished by having very good control of your power. When you project enough of your power outside your head and imitate hearing with power, you will actually get the physical feeling of hearing with your ear. When you use power to touch some object outside your body, your fingers will have an itchy feeling as if they were touching something lightly. This is a process of translation that your body is going through. When you use power to hear spiritual communication, you feel yourself hearing softly with your ear, and you also experience your power receiving words from the emanation of Power.

Take care that you can tell the difference between your thoughts and the transmissions of information through the ray of power. Your own thoughts will be inside your head and have a distinct vibration. They will seem very coarse by comparison. If you are in your power and remain there during the communication process, your mind and heart will be very silent, and no thoughts will occur in your mind. Words communicated to you through the ray of power will be subtle in vibration and will feel distinctly external. The words will have the feeling and vibration that you associate with the spiritual power that you are communicating with. You have to be able to distinguish your thoughts from the words that you are receiving along the channel. Your thoughts are definitely in your head. This is a key point.

The next level of accuracy in translating your communications from the spiritual emanation around you is to receive an image and then translate it. When you receive an image, it is generally because you are not ready to receive the message. You are not wanting to hear the message, and your mind turns the truth into a symbol so your conscious mind can accept it. Sometimes images are used because they are the best way for higher intelligence to communicate a very complex idea.

When you receive an image, it will be outside your head in the ray of power and will have the vibration of the emanation of power that you are communicating with. The image will have a distinctly real and solid feel to it. When you project your power out to touch the image, it will have a solidity and a concreteness to it. Your power will feel its solidity. This is a definite sign that you are dealing with something real to your power. If the image were manufactured by your brain it would disappear like a mirage when your power illumined it.

Images are very difficult to interpret. It is very easy for the mind to slip in and take control and change the meaning. Images must first be tested for reality, and then very quietly touched by power for their feeling. These feelings are not your emotions. They are subtle messages that come to you because you are listening and feeling with your power. Suddenly, as you are quietly feeling an image, you will know what is going on. Continue to feel the image and you will continue to get more intimations about what is going on. If you think about the image you will not translate it correctly. Your thoughts about the image will most likely totally distort the information that is conveyed to you by the image.

---

1. **EXTERNAL HEARING 75-100% ACCURATE**

2. **EXTERNAL FEELINGS 50-75% ACCURATE**

3. **EXTERNAL IMAGES 25% ACCURATE**

Communication techniques and their level of accuracy

When you get a series of feelings about what is going on in the image, ask for verbal communication and try to hear what the spiritual power has to tell you about the image. Getting feelings and verbal instructions about the image can give you very accurate information. Your image by itself without your mind will be about 25% accurate. Your feelings about the image will be 50-70% accurate. When you hear the emanation of Power externally at the end of your ray of power, the information will be 75-100% accurate. Many people find it very helpful to start with an image, get their feelings about it, and then get what their spiritual emanation says about it.

People who find it difficult to make verbal contact with a high spiritual intelligence can get fairly accurate information through images alone, but it is slow. Take the image given to you and get a very clear feeling about the image. Then take this first feeling, use it as if it were an image, and get another feeling. Use your power to get a second feeling, a feeling of the first feeling. The second feeling will be more accurate than the first feeling. When you get the second feeling, get the feeling of that feeling—the third feeling. Get deeper feelings until you suddenly find that the image you were seeing changes into something else. It is the last feeling before the image changes that you want to write down. You can disregard all the feelings before the last one. When the image changes, go for deeper and deeper feelings until you get the image to change. Generally, you will have to go no more than three levels deep, and it is the last feeling before the image changes that will give you the key words of the message that is being conveyed to you. You will find it helpful to write down each feeling or have someone write it down for you. You will find that what might take fifteen minutes to translate this way can be said in about five seconds. The biggest problem with this technique is that you will not want to go deeper. Your second feeling will still be saying the same thing as the first. You may have twenty similar descriptive feelings. A rock may feel hard, and hard may feel like a battle, and a battle may feel like a journey. If hard feels solid, then you are on the same level and are not going deeper.

When you have received your communication and translated accurately, you will then be able to receive confirmation from others about the accuracy of your translation. In a group of people who ask the same question, you will have strong confirmation that you have done your work accurately, because everyone in the group will get the same answer. Since this is real, there is no room for mistakes and confusion. If you are truly accessing higher intelligence, there must be confirmation. Ten people asking the same question will get the same answer.

ANOINTING: THE POWER AND THE ECSTASY

When you have learned to communicate with the emanation of Power that has drawn close to you, you can further your spiritual progress by learning how to commune with their spiritual vibration. This step rapidly alters your level of consciousness. By using your power to contact and commune with the spiritual embodiment of Power, you can taste the intelligence, bliss, and ecstasy that is the experience and existence of the highest spiritual Power. This experience begins the rapid spiritual transformation of both your physical body and your power.

Our goal is to become a perfected being, an incarnation of Power. For this to happen, your body and your power must both be transformed by the highest spiritual vibrations. Your entire being must become the spiritual vibrations of the highest power. Then you are transforming and healing not just your own being—you are also bringing true spiritual light into the world. You are radiating this light and power to others. You will become an incarnation of power, a perfected being.

Becoming an incarnation of power is a process in which you commune with the highest spiritual power, or an emanation of that power, and are transformed by that spiritual vibration into a new spiritual being. Previously, you extended your power out to make contact with your emanation of power so that you could communicate. Now you are going one step further. You will not only need to listen, but your entire body, mind, and power must be ready to allow the vibration of higher intelligence to manifest as a presence in you. You must be ready to experience the heightened states of consciousness and bliss that go along with wisdom and power. You cannot reach this state without establishing your communication with the higher powers of universal intelligence.

It is higher intelligence that will be guiding your spiritual journey, and you will need to begin listening to your higher intelligence if you are to progress at all. The major difficulty will be your fear of higher intelligence, a fear that will cause you to be unable to listen or be receptive. Previously, you only needed to be able to listen in order to access higher intelligence. Now, you will begin the systematic alteration of the vibrational field which you normally think of as your being. You will physically and psychologically change as your own power and body imbibe the spiritual vibrations of the spiritual emanation around you. It is like stepping into the sandals of the great beings of the past and experiencing the intelligence and bliss they felt as they walked the Earth. In this way you can jump ahead and quicken the pace of your spiritual development.

There are some very important reasons why this is so valuable for spiritual development. Whatever we do in our lives always takes place at the same level of growth. If we try and go on a spiritual path it never really leads anywhere. We tend to stay in the same ruts and never really change. At the end of your efforts you can't really say anything has happened. You may know more. You probably have gathered some new beliefs that control your life in a different way. You may have stopped eating meat, for example, or you may start wearing different clothes, or perhaps you have found new friends. Maybe you were lucky, and now you are a little calmer or less stressful. When you look deeply, though, there wasn't much change at all, and there wasn't much chance for you to change, because the experience wasn't real. It was just words. You believed in them and remained the same.

For you to change, you cannot feed your brain with some new theory, or change your clothes, friends, the way you talk or what you do, because it is just you doing all these things. For you to change, you have to drink from a different cup, and that cup cannot be your own, because you filled that cup yourself, and there is nothing in it that will change you. It *is* you. You made sure of that when you filled it. Instead, the very essence of your being, your power, has to undergo a radical change, and there is nothing you can do in the physical world to change power. You have to reach deep inside yourself and open to the highest power, and get a little help.

What we are talking about is a totally different experience, an experience that will not leave you exactly as you were before. It is a taste of the ecstasy of an incarnation of Power, and such a taste of love and ecstasy and power cannot leave you unchanged. For those who wish to move ahead on their spiritual path, to escape the trap of fear, this technique will allow them to fly as high as the angels, imbibe the bliss of Power, and forever know that this contracted fearful state is not their home.

The time has come when we can change the world. If enough people are willing to go forward and imbibe the vibrations of higher spiritual power and awareness, we can go forward. This world operates at a vibratory level that creates a very limited state of awareness, and the higher the vibration the closer this world is to a heaven. The way to immediately transform this world is for each of us to begin creating for him- or herself the highest spiritual vibration, and then we will be acting as a generator transmitting this high spiritual vibration to everyone that we meet. When there are many of these spiritual generators, the physical world will change, and the vibratory rate that keeps us bound to this level of limitation will lift, and true spiritual and material abundance will be ours.

At the present time the world doesn't understand what spirituality is. At the current level of intelligence most people are under the impression that being spiritual is an act of faith or belief. They think that if their beliefs are right, if they believe in the right god, or the right savior or prophet, then they are spiritual. This is more like business or politics than spirituality. Their religion is in their mind, it's not real. When they listen to speeches about morality or religion, they may feel moved, and the more they are moved by the speech the more spiritual they think they have become. This is more like entertainment than spirituality. This level of mentality can have a holy war and see it as a spiritual act.

This level of intelligence is caused by fear and contraction. When your power narrows to become just a tiny fragment of itself, you become totally identified with your thoughts. If you are thinking about something spiritual, you feel that you are spiritual. When you have a belief or a habit that you've been told is spiritual, you think you are spiritual because you have this habit. In this contracted state we are asleep in a dream, and we think our dream is real. We have lost our ability to contact the world around us, and we have lost our ability to contact our own higher intelligence. We see only our thoughts, and we think we see the world.

Our inability to recognize anything real is just the intelligence of a particular vibratory level. The solidity and materiality of this world are just your power's descent into lower vibratory levels, just as your genius and experience of freedom will be your ascent into the higher vibrations of spirituality.

It is through this technique of power that you bring spiritual vibrations into the world. Your power, your mind, and your body will begin changing and ascending to the heights of spirituality. When you have done this for yourself, the people around you will begin changing. Their own state will be brought to a higher level, as if by electrical induction. The higher power will pass from one person to the other and finally everyone will have been touched and the journey will begin.

The technique, while simple, becomes difficult because of the fear involved. Even mentioning fear makes it harder for you to do it. It is easiest if you don't know what you are doing. All techniques of power can be done by anyone as long as they don't know what they are doing. If it's a game, and doesn't mean anything, anybody can do it. When you know what you are doing and realize its significance, you block yourself. You become frightened, and suddenly, you freeze. Things you could do before you cannot do, and you wonder where your skill has gone. Nothing has happened to your skill. You have shrunk from the light.

When you feel comfortable communicating with high spiritual intelligence, you can allow your body, mind, and power to become affected by the highest spiritual vibration. You should already know the position of the spiritual emanation around you.

The first process is easiest if you choose a place that is on the opposite side of your body from the spiritual emanation, about a foot or so away. If the spiritual emanation is on your left side, choose a place on the right side. This is the direction that you will move. You should make contact with the emanation around you, and then you should send another beam of your power to the place you have chosen. If you are just starting out, you will not want to go very far with this ray of your power. You will then move however

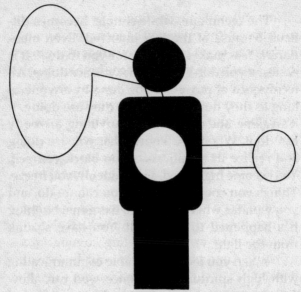

Step 1: Communing with an Emanation of Power

much of your power in this direction as you wish.

The next step is to again contact your spiritual emanation. While tracing the channel from that spirit to your own power and sending a beam of your own power back out to them, you contact them and invite them close to you. Feel the close proximity and inform them that you are going to step out and you'd like them to step in. Then, while maintaining your connection to this Power, project as much of your power as possible to the place you have chosen. You want to feel as though you are a little displaced.

You will have the feeling of being in two places at once. Your eyes will be seeing from your body, but you won't feel that you are looking out of them. You then want to invite the high spiritual force to come into your body. You can feel and see the occurrence from your power that is projected to the right. This transfer can happen slowly or very quickly. When you get the knack of doing it quickly, it feels as if a rotation has taken place. Suddenly, you have moved right, and the emanation is in.

There is still some of your power remaining in your physical body, and you immediately begin to feel the most exquisite feeling coming into your body. After a few minutes your body will feel like it has never felt before. You are weightless, there is no pain, and you begin to feel that your body is floating in space and is ethereal, like a mirage. You feel your center is displaced to the side as a bystander, but you are still firmly in control and experiencing what it is to live in the ecstasy of a high spiritual power.

Although your body may appear to physically change, and your voice may change with the entry of new vibrations, you are still in control. You don't lose control. Nothing will be making you say or do things. You are just imbibing the spiritual vibrations of the emanation of power that is near you.

Your communications with this spiritual intelligence will be different than before. Pre-

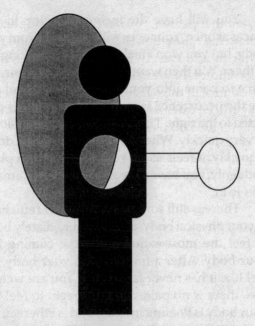

Step 2: Communing with an Emanation of Power

viously you heard the communications occurring outside your body. Now they are inside
your body, but you are outside, hearing them.
You switched places. You are listening from outside your body, and what you hear them say will
be inside you, but there will be a distance. To accurately get the message, you have to listen carefully and not translate. You want to get the
message word for word. This is a key point, because your fear will want to change the meaning
and the exact sense of it. To convey any message

to another person, you have to step aside and just allow the repetition of the words to come out of your mouth exactly as you hear them with no alterations. You don't want to think that you are in control of the wisdom, and that whatever you say will be true. You are not yet a spiritual power, so you are still listening, not talking.

Step 3: Communing with an Emanation of Power

After you have studied at that level for a while, you will want to try staying inside of your body while the spiritual emanation comes into your body. Your power and their power will occupy the same space. You will be more fully transformed by the spiritual vibrations, and their power will have greater impact on your spiritual growth. It may be difficult communicating accurately without some experience, because there is no distance between you. For transformation, though, this technique allows you to imbibe the vibrations and be transformed without the disorientation of moving your power outside your body. In this way the full impact of the transformation will be available whenever you want it.

THE INCARNATION
OF POWER

*T*he dream of humanity throughout time and throughout all religions has been to regain our lost heritage, to regain the lost power, wisdom, and beauty that deep in our being we know we possess. We know in our hearts that this material world is not our home, that it is not fulfilling our deepest desires. Within our being is the wisdom, the power, and the light to break through the physical barrier that is the crystallization of our fear and contraction. We have lost our highest wisdom and have inherited a world that, because of our fear, our ignorance, and our lack of freedom, does not satisfy.

If we can understand the light and power within us, if we can feel that we are spiritual beings of light and power, and can recognize and use our spiritual wisdom, then we will at last fulfill the dreams of mankind and bring the light and wisdom that religions have talked about into the world. We will have joined the family of Power. We will have regained our lost heritage, as well as our wisdom and power, and will begin to transform this world into the paradise that is truly our home. The destiny of the world will be in the hands of the family of Power, who are communing with the highest spiritual Power. With wisdom we will understand our highest purpose and the highest purpose of mankind. With Power we will create not only our own future but the future of the world. We will create humankind's true inheritance. The techniques of power will enable you to gain the highest wisdom and to learn to create and control your personal future and the future of mankind. The techniques of power will be available to all who reawaken to their own divinity and discover the power that is their own higher intelligence. We will create a family of awakened beings, beings who have the wisdom and the power to create the destiny that we have always wanted.

To understand the process of reawakening to your divinity, you should understand the process that has lead to your limited consciousness. Your power is a small fragment of the universal power and light that is the summit of the second level of existence. Your individual power and light is like a drop of water in a great ocean of light. It is of the same substance, but it is cut off and separate. How does the separation take place?

How does the drop lose its home? Your power has become habituated and fixated to a contracted viewpoint, which causes it to be unaware of its home and to live in a dream. It stares too long and has become engrossed in the physical world, and the dream has become very real and heavy. As the dream becomes more real, your viewpoint becomes more and more narrow, until your power becomes a cramped little ball of energy. When you have become habituated and addicted to the narrow viewpoint, you become fearful about losing the contraction. The pain of the contraction becomes so familiar that any loss of contraction causes fear. The whole state of being is just fear and contraction. Our human consciousness is created with waves of contracting energy. At the point of total contraction there is the explosion of human awareness which obliterates the feeling of contraction that preceded it. But there are spaces between the explosions of human consciousness, and there are spaces between the preceding contractions. In the space, your consciousness does not exist. There is no consciousness. You don't feel that your mind is flickering on and off, that it is a series of endless waves— but it is. This fact is used in the martial arts of the East. You can watch a person and get his rhythm. His movements, the blinking of his eyes, each gesture begins at the time his mind becomes conscious, at the time the explosion of human consciousness occurs. This is when he can act; the rest of the time he is unconscious and vulnerable. By watching and knowing the opponent's rhythm, you can act when he is not conscious—when he cannot act—and then you can easily win the battle.

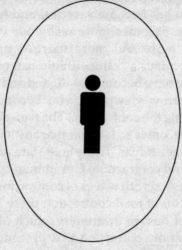

The Expanded State of Power

In a similar fashion we are going into battle to be victorious over the mind. It is the continued contraction of our power that is the root cause of all fear. By practicing the art of expanding the power, and by expanding it into the universe, we become more and more familiar with the state of transcendence, and the state of not being trapped within the human condition—the condition of fear and contraction. If we were able to maintain the power in its fully expanded state, there would be no fear and contraction. With the absence of fear and contraction (the dawning of the state of Power), you have perfected power and become an incarnation of Power. You are then released from the limited viewpoint of a body that dies.

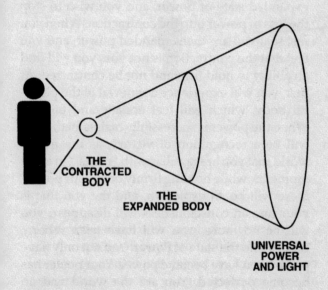

The Contraction of Universal Power and Light

When you are in the expanded state, your power can witness the contraction into the human mechanism. From this height, what you had experienced as fear is seen only as contraction. You can see how the contraction of your power is sucking the power and light into a vortex that creates the human consciousness and the world. When you see this, and you see the limitation and uselessness of it all, you want to remain in the expanded state of power, and you wish to stop the loss of power into the contraction. When you feel that you are that expanded power, and you feel that the contraction is not you, you will find an ability to hold firm and not be contracted. At first, you will experience a renewal of the physical body, which will feel ecstatic and blissful. When the power is successfully maintained, there will be a recognition of victory, as the mind/world that you are familiar with "melts." In a few moments, while holding firmly onto your power, there will be an explosion, and the you that is your human consciousness will disappear; you will be no more. You will have been reborn, reborn into the state of Power. You not only have power, you have become power. Your power has become perfected. You are the world and an incarnation of Power.

You are not required to become a spiritual giant to access or use your power. You can recognize your spiritual essence and begin ending the fear and contraction that creates your limitation.

You can use your higher intelligence and change your life and the world. You can tap your power and contact the highest spiritual sources in the universe. You will fully understand your life, and your power will guide you toward the creation of your highest spiritual and material destiny. The first goal is to discover within ourselves the vast light and power that is our essence. We will then begin to see that we are not just a physical body, and that our life and our human destiny is not dominated and controlled by these physical limitations. We will discover a whole new realm of existence that is the very foundation of this world. When you have perceived your own essence and power, you will begin using your creative wisdom to harmonize your life with the deeper forces that dominate the physical world, and you will begin to understand your place and your future within the grand design. The discovery of your place, your destiny, and your fulfillment is an extraordinary development. It is like nothing else in this world.

The dreams and hopes of the average person are based on the idea that one will live forever, and that this physical world and its pleasures are all there is to life. These mad dreams have nothing to do with reality and come from a person's fear and contraction. A person of fear and contraction will only create more confusion and contraction no matter how lofty their dreams. It is only when we begin to act from our higher intelligence that we begin to see through the veil and operate from a different level of reality. When a person becomes acquainted with the truth, he or she recognizes it as being beyond the dream. Our higher intelligence is the creative wisdom and the power of the universe. Our normal state of consciousness is in total opposition to this creative force. It operates in denial of our higher nature. Our conscious mind is what is left of our consciousness after we have contracted with fear from the intelligence, light, and power of our deepest nature. Any activity that begins from the level of fear and contraction will be in direct opposition to the creative forces of nature. This activity cannot be successful and will be self-defeating no matter how successful it may appear. How would it be possible for a person to deny his own higher intelligence and power and expect to be successful in his own life? It is only by being able to go beyond the limitations of the deep fear and contraction that has limited our awareness that we can understand what is best for our lives. Then, with higher intelligence, we can access the real power of creation and change our own lives by creating those things that will really fulfill us. When you become capable of reaching beyond your own fear and contraction, you will be able to achieve and create your life's purpose. First you have to learn what the contraction is. Then you learn the techniques to reach beyond. When you have reached beyond, you will want to discover the truth about yourself. The truth is not something you want to hear. If you wanted to hear the truth, you would already be perfectly aware. You must be able to step around the constant fear and contraction to find the truth, the truth that we have denied and buried in the corners of our being.

Each of you will have the choice of standing in the light of higher intelligence or withdrawing into the shadows to keep your secret motives from being destroyed in the light. Your secret motives are based on your fear and contraction and can only be nourished if you remain asleep. If you were able to see your secret motives (by not obscuring the truth with noisy thoughts which narrow the mental capacity), you would reject them as the basis for your life. The limited mind is harboring a life purpose that is so deviant that you would not want it within you if you could see it. That is why you cannot see it. It has been buried beneath many layers of noise in your mind. By a higher intelligence that is not based on your mechanical brain or your fear, your real life's purpose can be discovered and consciously created.

When you have found your power and seen through the veil of fear, your life's purpose will fuel your life. You will find others whose life purposes harmonize with yours. Your life's purpose is your share in the fulfillment of humanity, and together with others you will discover and create a greater purpose. The family of Power will find that together they have more intelligence and power than they have separately. They will be able to aid one another in their self-discovery and in the discovery of the greater family purpose.

This will be the beginning of the material fulfillment of the family of Power. The formation of the family of Power and its highest purpose is the great force needed to change the world. Spiritually fearless people will begin discovering their own true identity and power. These powerful individuals will then use their power to create their own futures in accordance with higher intelligence. The world will be a flexible medium of power, and will bend and alter itself to accommodate the creation of the higher purposes of these individuals. The world in its highest sense has been wanting to create something higher than the impotent, fear-based dreams of the common person and will dramatically begin propelling these individuals to their higher destiny. These creators of the future will unite in their creative efforts and begin discovering and creating the higher family purpose.

The higher family purpose is the vision of the family's greatest gift to humanity. Their power benefits themselves and benefits the world. There is greater power at work, greater than the power of one individual, and this creative power will affect the lives of many people. There has never been a time or an opportunity for such rapid powerful changes to take place for so many people. This is the miracle: that you can be empowered, and that you can create your spiritual and material fulfillment. Then you can help create the spiritual and material fulfillment of the world.

The family of power will create the future and cause the light in the world to grow. The power and light of the One will be spread silently throughout the world. The natural and spontaneous work of the family will be to act as a giant Power generator. Fear and contraction will not be found in the family of Power, and their light will silently pass to others who will find themselves less contracted and more spiritual. In their own way and in their own time the delusions and the twisted logic of fear will begin to fade away, and the unconscious children of light will fall away from the fear-based patterns of their normal lives and be drawn to higher intelligence and higher purpose.

The generation of light and power will cause those who want to know the truth to celebrate a growing light in the world. Those who, as Jesus said, "hate the light because their deeds are evil" will still need to come to the light. The goal is to bring the light into the world and into the lives of all people, so that heaven can be found at our fingertips and not in some far-distant, post-mortem fantasy world. This requires freedom from the fear that comes when you bring the light of

Power into your life and the world. The family of Power will create a future for humanity free of the fear and contraction that is the cause of this level of consciousness. Fear will be lifted and there will be a spiritual transformation in the world, so that the contraction of universal power and light that has brought us to the level of bestiality will turn and raise us to the level of spiritual enlightenment on a planetary scale.

CREATING THE FUTURE

*T*he future of humanity is in the hands of those who can create the future. The future is not a fixed format. You are directing the show, and it is your skill in using your power that will decide your future. Because of your fear and contraction, you are creating a future that you don't really want. You have already chosen a path, but don't know where it is leading. You have a habit and are already stuck, and there may be no escape. You may stumble over a cliff blindly and not even know how you did it. The family of Power will stand by and watch, but they can do nothing. It was your choice. If you decide to keep your fear, it will destroy you. Your fear is hard to face, but until you face it, you will stumble along your own way.

To create your best future is not an impossible dream. You don't have to be trapped. You can go a different way, a way that will fulfill your highest goals. There is a path that leads back to your home, and it is filled with the joys of adventure. You can go safely on the journey that will benefit you the most. When you face your fear, it is an easy journey, and your opportunity to have everything you really want. If you fearlessly set your course, it is easily followed. The vessel you have will take you there.

How do you set the course? You need help; you can't do it alone. It takes people. Your goals are the goals of the many. No man is an island, and involving others will bring your success. You cannot be successful alone. There are networks of people who will be helping to create the future. Each person will have his share in the vision, which will be created by the many. This network of people will be creating a collective future, and will advance spiritually and materially. Their vision will spread and new people will find their place in the vision. Humanity is not made up of separate individuals. Each person is a piece of a whole, and when the power and the vision lifts you spiritually and materially, all of humanity will be affected.

Like any vessel, your ship needs a star to sail her by. Your star will not be your star alone. It will be a piece of the master plan for all humanity, and it will be your highest purpose in this life. It will be the purpose that will fulfill your innermost dreams, and your innermost dreams will be a part of a greater overall dream, a dream that will be the highest purpose of humanity. This vision will be humanity's fulfillment.

The people who create their highest future are the people who will be creating the destiny of mankind. They will have mastered power and the techniques of power, and together they will create their own destiny and the destiny of the world. They will do this because, as a part of the family of power, they have access to the highest power and intelligence in the universe, and they have been given the power to create their vision in the physical world.

Having mastered power and the techniques of power, you will use your power to help people. You can help the world the most by not being confused. If you are not clear about the direction of your life, if you are not clear about your highest purpose, you will not be fulfilled, and you will not be fulfilling the vision of higher intelligence. You will not benefit yourself, and you will not benefit humanity as a whole. There is a place for you in the family of enlightened humanity and a place among the people who are creating the future. If your highest future is not fulfilled, then humanity is fulfilled that much less. You are not an island, and we are doing this together.

Your ability to use the techniques of power will enable you to discover what part of the future you need to create. As you begin learning the techniques of power, you will begin to learn about yourself. You will begin to learn about the spiritual side of yourself, and that what you have treasured as you is only a fragment of the real you and is not the source of either your intelligence or your power. Once you have seen this fact and begin releasing your mind and power from the grip of fear and contraction, you can investigate the vision that you need to create in order to assume your place among the creators of the future.

Fear has been the only thing holding you back, and fear will be the only thing to hold you back in the future. Your power knows your proper place and your highest purpose, and its higher intelligence is not far from you. You have heard its words, and your fear has caused you to shrink from it; now to avoid the truth you are doing anything except what you deeply want to do. It is by being open to higher intelligence, by asking, listening, and trusting, that you will understand your part in the future of this world.

The wisdom of your power body provides the easiest way to discover your highest purpose. This wisdom can be used for the discovery of the worldly aspects of your life's purpose. If an emanation of the highest power has drawn close to you, and you can communicate, it will give you the best spiritual information. Using the wisdom of your own power is the easiest of all the techniques of power to master. Almost everybody

has the ability to master the technique very quickly, and because of its accuracy and ease of use with worldly affairs, this is the easiest and fastest way to find out in what direction your life should be going.

The technique is very simple (you should have a piece of paper and a pen to write down the information). First, you should get into your power at the center of your being. Put an image of yourself in your mind. With the light and power from your center, illumine the image of yourself and ask what your highest purpose should be. Illumine and watch the image, your feelings, and your thoughts. You will begin to get some amazing facts about yourself, your future, and the areas of life that you should begin investigating. Be very silent inside. You may see images that will convey certain feelings or meanings to you. You should do this several times to get more and more detail about your purpose and to verify that what you receive is valid.

The interpretation of the images is the most sensitive area. Here's an example. You see an image of the ocean with rocks and trees and waves. You immediately think of a place where you have been on a similar coastline where you would like to live, and you want to think that power is telling you to live there. It is probably not. As soon as you saw the image you jumped into your mind and your memory and decided that you would like to live there. Interpreting takes some care and experience so that you don't try to translate everything in terms of your past experiences. Remember that the images are not what is important. The image is your brain's way of allowing your conscious mind to accept higher intelligence without threat. You have to have care and patience to allow your wisdom to shine through. You have to translate the image accurately.

You need to take your power and illumination and carefully feel the image, while remaining silent. Make sure you are centered in your power and very silent. Your feelings will tell you more of the truth than will the image itself. Your feelings will tell you what is going on in the image. Be aware that as you get information that you feel is significant, you may want to leave your power and jump into fear. You may immediately jump into your mind, and not even realize it. Remember that the only reason that you don't already have this wisdom is because you have fearfully shut down your higher intelligence. You must be careful that you don't fool yourself. If you have someone do it with you, and you both get the same information, then you have a good verification that you have done well.

As you develop your power techniques, you will see that your power and light must clear the mind of the unreal in order to get accurate information and higher intelligence. If the mind is not cleansed of the false, and if the higher intelligence is not the source of the images in the brain, then the images that you perceive will have no wisdom, no substance, and no power. It is this important fact about power and its application that you have to fully understand when you put it to use. Without understanding power and the images that power creates as opposed to the images the brain creates, there is only confusion and no fundamental way to create the future with any kind of control. You will not know whether you are creating anything real or just dreaming.

After you have successfully laid out your highest purpose, you can use your power to begin creating it. To create the future, you need to experience the power at the center of your being very strongly. You must have the ability to illumine the brain with your light and power. When you have a clear image of your higher purpose, and you can illuminate it, touch it, feel it, and understand it with your power, then you have laid the foundation.

You need to send a ray of your power to touch the image and very carefully begin building each piece of the image. You have to permeate the image with your power and feel your power becoming the material that the image is made of. Carefully build the entire image with your power so that it no longer feels like an image that you are looking at so much as an image that you have become. Project as much of your power into building the image as you can, until you feel that it is you.

As you progress in your spiritual development and begin going beyond the wisdom of your own power body, you will begin using the highest spiritual intelligence available to you. Your highest purpose will be given to you by the emanation of Power that is given to you. The intelligence of your own power, although it is a fragment of universal intelligence, does not possess the full power and intelligence of the whole. The fragmentation that created your power comes from fear and contraction and a denial of the highest intelligence. Using your own power will not give you the wisdom and intelligence of the higher spiritual sources.

It is the emanations of Power that will really propel your creative capacities. Not only will you be getting complete wisdom about your purpose, but you will be working in close harmony with the greatest powers in the universe. These great powers do not interfere in your life. It is your life and your own development, and it is your decision whether to grow or not, just as it has been your choice so far not to listen to your own higher intelligence. The emanations of Power are very willing to give those rare souls who wish to turn to the light everything they need to create their highest purpose. To create your highest future with their help, you do not have just the limited power and intelligence of your own power and light. For your highest future you have the power and intelligence of the highest Power in the universe, a power which your soul is a contracted form of.

When you have the ability to communicate and commune with an emanation of Power, that spiritual power will give you the knowledge of what you need to create. Just as you used the wisdom of your power to discover your purpose, now you will use your communication skills with your emanation of Power to find out where you should go in your life. When you are clear about the direction, you can begin the process of creating your future.

Creation takes place when you use your power to build the image for yourself. Your teacher will have given you an image of what you need to create. Send a ray of your power out to the image and use your power to also create the image. When you have co-created the image to the point where it feels as if it were you, then you have set in motion the creation of the future. Within a very short time you will notice the world starting to go in the direction that you have created with your power.

There will be some circumstances or developments that you will notice within a short time. Actually the creation and change in the world has already been initiated, but it may take a little while for you to notice. Within a couple of days

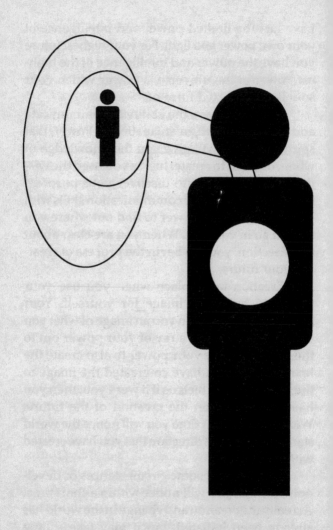

The Power to Create

you should notice some development. If you do not notice a change, it is either because you did not do the technique correctly or you just did not notice the new development. Either way, try again and stay alert, because the good news is on the way.

Creating the future with an emanation of Power has more power than creating the future with your own power. When you create using an emanation, you are acting from a level of consciousness which your current level of spiritual advancement cannot not attain. You are accessing a level of intelligence and power that you personally will probably not reach for some time.

Your own power has its limitations, because your mind loves to take control. Using your power is the first step in spiritual development. It is the easiest step because it arouses the least fear. You feel like you have control, so it causes the least threat to the mind and if you start to lose control, you can just distort things and fool yourself. With the distortion caused by fear, you will lose power and create illusions and your creative powers will not work for you.

When you have seen the truth of your ability to create the future, what will you do with the power? The right step is to discover your highest purpose. The power should be used to fulfill the highest purposes and dreams of every person, both in a spiritual and material way. All the techniques of power have but one goal. They are designed to first end the fear and contraction that has caused us to fall from our highest wisdom and power. This is the key to our spiritual growth. We need to create a future where we are free of fear and contraction and have recognized our true spiritual core. Secondly we need to take care of our material world and create abundance for ourselves and the world. Each person must learn how to discover and create their highest purpose. Then the world will have abundance. Spirituality without material abundance has no power, and material abundance without spirituality has no intelligence. We must create a spiritually and materially abundant world. We must radically transform the planet into the spiritual garden that it can be.

THE VISION

The ultimate use of power is to benefit the world. No man is an island, and as you grow in your spiritual awareness, you will realize that you are the world and that you are a member of the family of power. This vision will become unshakable, and at the height of your awareness you will live as the world and as the family of power. You will be acting from the universal power and light that is the foundation of the world. You will tap your highest wisdom and intelligence, and you will advance the spiritual and material evolution of humanity.

The family of power is dedicated to the spiritual and material advancement of humanity, and its wisdom and power will help fulfill that vision. The wisdom is the wisdom of the highest and the power is the ability to manifest that wisdom into our physical reality. The ultimate goal of wisdom and power on the personal level is to become an incarnation of Power. The family's members are the ones who have become the universal power and light and have full access to the spiritual powers. When you become such a one, power and the techniques of power are in your nature and not something special.

Power's primary concern is to put you on the track of both your spiritual and material fulfillment, so that you can be of benefit to the world. As you spiritually advance, you will be bringing the power and light into your life and into the world. Your power and light will transform your own life and will be transmitted to those around you. You will begin to see that as you are benefitting yourself, you are benefitting others. You are no longer concerned about yourself, but just want to be of help.

Power and the techniques of power become yours because you have advanced beyond the fear and contraction of your life. This is power. The techniques of power give you the wisdom to understand, from spiritual heights, where you need to go and what you need to do. They give you the spiritual power to control the physical reality so that your spiritual and material paths begin materializing before you. This will be the vision of the individual of power. When you discover the primary mission of your life, you will access the highest wisdom and power. You will lead the life of a perfected being, and it will be the most fulfilling thing that you can do.

As you create your highest life purpose with power you will be joining the family of Power. You are a part of the family of Power by your connection to the ultimate Power and by the part you play in the ultimate vision for the world. Power's highest vision of the world will become your vision, and you will have the spiritual power to create the future which will be humanity's highest achievement.

The family of power is the doorway to the transformation of the world. The family of power will be advancing spiritually and materially, and we will be creating the future which the vision of our highest purpose directs. We realize that we are the world. We are not alone and we want to be of help. Our profound impulse will be the foundation for the great quantum leap, the coming of light and power into the world. We will create the highest spiritual and material fulfillment for ourselves and, as the family of Power, we will create the highest future for the world. The spiritual light of the family of Power will generate a force that will penetrate the veil of the world and elevate humanity.

The family of power, dedicated to your spiritual and material advancement, will provide a foundation for your growth. There is always a tendency for the mind to doubt what is gained through higher intelligence. The mind that is trapped in fear and contraction doubts anything that is higher; but if you doubt or are shocked by something, it is probably true. The reason you don't already have greater wisdom is because you don't want to hear it. It takes a special effort to allow your higher intelligence to come into your life. Having a family of friends who share your vision will allow you to trust your higher intelligence. When you have many friends whose higher intelligence confirms yours, then you can more easily believe what you cannot see.

The family of power will give strength to your spiritual and material transformation. It will give you the energy to do more than you could do alone. The power of the group will provide a perfect place for your growth to happen. The family will put you back in contact with your highest intelligence so that you can redirect your life toward your highest goals. Your family of friends will help you understand the direction of your life and help you clarify and create your life purpose.

As you create your life purpose, you will find friends whose life purposes mesh with yours. Your life purpose will connect with another's, and together you will be creating a greater future. You will find friends who have a common vision, and the common vision will create a special family of power. The special family of power will be people of high spiritual character using their highest intelligence and acting together to create a special vision. Groups of such people will clarify and create the special family's higher purpose, just as individuals have clarified their highest purpose. These special family purposes will be the way groups of people are benefitted.

Special families concerned with business will form so that the life purposes that involve businesses will flourish. The special business family will use the highest intelligence and power to create the futures of their businesses. People interested in politics will gather together to influence the course of politics. People interested in the course of organized religion may want to gather to influence the course of religion. There will be scientists who will want to use power for scientific purposes. People interested in healing will be healing and discovering new healing techniques. There will be ten thousand groups with as many different special purposes.

The vision of the future is of a world of people who have gone beyond war, hunger, and suffering and are able to unite as one spiritual power to bring wisdom into the world. The ultimate spiritual benefit to mankind is ending the state of fear and contraction in human consciousness and the attainment of global enlightenment. The ultimate material benefit for mankind is to have every person know and attain his highest and most fulfilling life purpose and to achieve the magnificent abundance available to them. This will be the beginning of the family of people who control the destiny of the world.

It depends on you. It depends on your ability to listen, to love, and to spiritually advance. It depends on your ability to perfect your power, and to overcome your fear. If you have the power to create the future and can fulfill your life's purpose, you have begun to help. When you experience the ecstasy of communion with the great emanations of Power and taste the calm, still waters of Power, you will create the spiritual and material revolution.

DISCIPLINE

You can do nothing without discipline. On any path there is a first step, a last step, and every step in between. Each step follows the others, and if you never take your first step, you'll never see your goal. If you never take your last step, you'll never reach the end. Dreams are dreams until you decide to make them real. Whatever you decide to do, you'll need to do it. You'll need to gather all your courage and commitment to make your highest visions come true. Discipline comes from your commitment to your highest purpose and allows you to ignore the temporary setbacks and fears, giving you the strength to keep putting one foot in front of the other until you have reached your goal. Do what is best for you, and never stop.

APPENDIX

Entering the Power Body:

Step-by-Step Instructions

I. Begin by becoming very familiar with the concepts in the chapter "Fear and Contraction." Continue to periodically read the chapter and observe yourself and others.

A. Understand how the three levels of existence relate to contraction and fear.

B. Make a commitment to yourself to understand how fear is operating in your life. Keep a notebook or journal of your progress. Write out your commitments.

C. Read and fully understand the three levels of fear. From the symptoms, estimate where you are among the three levels of fear. You may be halfway between levels two and three, for example.

D. Read and understand intellectually the dynamics of how fear creates thought and the subconscious mind. Write down in your journal your understanding of the concept.

1. Experiment and discover how hearing takes place. When you hear a sound, notice that there is a recognition of it before you become conscious of it. Your mind recreates the sound or words to become conscious of them. Write your experiences in a journal.
2. Write down ways in which your mind distorted things in this re-creation.
3. Write down the difference between the experience of the simple recognition of words and the experience of these words after your mind has repeated the words.

E. Find out how often you use the noise of thought to block intelligence.

1. Take ten minutes and write down every thought that comes into your mind. What did you think about? How important was it that you were thinking about those things at that time? Did you find anything of importance? During how much time was your mind silent? Continue to do this experiment daily, until you see how your mind is working.
2. Discover how much of your day is consumed in thought and keep records of this in your journal.
3. Discover how and why you are spending so much time thinking and bring it to a stop. Write down your progress.

F. Find examples in yourself of how fear creates thought, and describe this in a notebook. Watch how your wisdom grows as you progress.

   1. Your fear surrounds your secret motive, your lower life purpose. Discover the repeated patterns of your fear and describe them. Become familiar with your fear patterns.

   2. When you have become familiar with your fear patterns, begin to go deeper and witness your own secret motive that causes those fears to exist.

   3. It may be helpful to find others who have your same commitment who can help you discover your fears and secret motives.

   4. Watch for differences between what you say and what you do.

   5. List the problem areas of your life, and watch for and list all the fears related to each area that occur. Watch for the secret motive. Be objective.

G. Practice listening to other people, giving them the time to express their ideas. Watch how you respond to them and how they respond to you. Describe what you find.

   1. Find and describe examples of how others are not listening to you so much as listening to their own thoughts.

2. Find examples of your doing the same thing. You may need a friend to help.

3. Find examples of others' distorting what is said to them. Get familiar with how it happens.

4. Find examples of your distorting what is said to you. Get help if you can't find any.

5. List every occasion of someone's saying something to you that made you angry or upset. Find out why you were upset and write it down.

H. Find and describe examples of people who manage fear by creating fantasy worlds and fantasy personalities. Your ability to see this occurring will mark your progress in listening.

1. Discover and describe the times when you have also done this. Write down the circumstances around the time someone thought you did this.

I. Find examples of truth entering your mind and record it in your journal. Note when, where, and how it happened.

1. Find times and places where you can be quiet and still, where you can feel a natural joy and intelligence.

2. Notice and write down how your mind becomes quiet and how it becomes noisy.

II. Read and become familiar with the chapter "Techniques of Power." Continue to read it periodically.
   A. Understand the conscious, unconscious, and subconscious states. Describe your new understandings.

III. Periodically read the chapters "The Mind and the Power," "The Body of Power," and "The Wisdom of Power." Describe your understandings.
   A. Do the first experiment in "The Mind and the Power" and describe your discoveries. This experiment should be done regularly until it is a normal part of your experience.
      1. Relax and shut your eyes. Notice your state of consciousness. Describe the difference in consciousness while your eyes are open and closed. Become familiar with how much of your consciousness depends on your ability to see. Write down exactly what percentage of your total consciousness seeing constitutes.
      2. With your eyes shut, notice your thoughts. Listen to them, and notice what they are. Say your name in your brain. Say your name out loud. What is the difference? Describe your experiences.

3. Determine what percentage of your consciousness is made up of the sounds in your brain. Determine what percentage of your consciousness is left without sight and the ability to think.

B. Quiet the mind for perception. Describe all experiences.

1. Shut your eyes and relax the body. Experiment with different relaxation techniques. Find the one that relaxes you the best. Keep records.

2. Note what happens when you keep your body absolutely still. Make notes of the changes.

3. Note what happens when you keep your eyes absolutely still. Make notes of the changes.

4. Find out what awareness is.

(a) Stare at an object. Note the distance.

(b) Visualize the tree in your mind. Note the distance. Where is your awareness? Aren't the tree outside and the tree inside objects of awareness?

(c) Describe why you don't recognize that reality in your everyday life. What process occurs that causes you to feel like you are the voices and images in your mind?

(d) Continue this experiment daily until you no longer feel that you are the thoughts and images in your mind.

(e) Describe what awareness is.

IV. Read the chapter "The Body of Power" periodically and understand the concepts.

A. Write in your journal experiences when you may have felt weightless, or felt an incredible joy or peace come to you for no reason. Continue to describe such experiences.

   1. Has a sight of incredible beauty ever brought your mind to a stop, bringing a feeling of profound peace and joy?

B. Write down what it feels like to be very tired and sitting in a soft chair. What are the physical feelings? Did you notice your thinking stop? Did you experience a sinking feeling, physical pleasure, or peace? Can you feel where you are centered? Can you feel the feeling of not being centered behind the eyes in the head?

C. Get familiar with the feeling of thinking, of being centered behind the eyes in your head. See if you can compare it to the sinking feeling you get when you relax.

D. After studying the chapter, write down your understanding of the benefits of being centered in your power rather than in your mind.

E. Describe every experience you have of being centered in the head and having your center drop or sink.

V. Read the chapter "Wisdom of tthe Power Body" regularly and understand and practice the principles described there.

A. Practice your preparation techniques.

1. Practice your relaxation technique.

2. Still your body, your eyes, and your mind.

B. Going beyond your thoughts.

1. Practice the technique of noticing your hearing. Record the results of your experiences.

(a) Very quietly, very gently notice the hearing. An act of mild attention. Practice this.

(b) Note the difference between listening to sounds and noticing the hearing. Listening causes the mind to repeat the sounds that are heard. Noticing the hearing is a very quiet act. Can you tell the difference? Describe the difference.

(c) As you continue to notice the hearing you will notice a peace coming to your body and mind that was not there before. The whole world will seem quieter. Practice this and note the experiences of your success in your journal.

(d) After you have felt the quietness come over you and your mind is silent, begin noticing softer and softer sounds. Take several minutes and notice softer and softer sounds.

(e) After several minutes, find the softest sound you can find. Take several minutes.

(f) Now look closely and see if your breath is the softest sound you have heard. Have you heard your heartbeat?

(g) Can you hear a silence?

2. You should be able to note several distinct changes in your consciousness. They are indications that you have entered your power body that you will need to look for. Write them down in your journal.

(a) The senses will have changed in a very unique way: Your hearing will not feel like normal hearing. It will feel like feeling. If your eyes are shut, your hearing will feel very much like feeling. You must be able to get this feeling, or you have probably not entered your power. (Your power merges all the senses into one.)

(b) Your center of focus or the feeling of "me" will have shifted: (1) Your center will have sunk into your body near the heart or stomach area. Some people feel a warmth there. (2) You will have the definite sensation that you are not looking with your eyes, but from behind your eyes. Your vision will start from your center. (3) You should notice a separation from your thoughts when they occur. They will not have power over you. (4) You should not feel the strong feeling of "I" as the body. You will have a feeling of being connected with the world. (5) Write down any other changes that you notice.

3. The most important practice is to not make this a special thing that is done occasionally. You should be able to fairly quickly master the art of being in this state throughout the day.

(a) In your journal, keep track of when you enter your power and the symptoms of this in the beginning.

(b) Later you should do it during the day: (1) Start by doing it at breaks in your day. (2) Next, do it while you are listening to someone. (3) Try it while working. Just start noticing your hearing all day and get used to the feeling. (4) Especially do it in your relationships. Keep records of your experiences in your journal.

(c) Keep records of how much of your day is spent in your power. Keep track of how much of your day is spent in your thoughts. Note that you can still think in your power, but your relationship with your thoughts is far more distant.

4. When you are almost always in your power, and you don't spend your time thinking and talking to yourself, you can finally listen. You have escaped the three levels of fear. Congratulations!

PSIONIC POWER
by Charles Cosimano

Can a machine really amplify one's psychic powers? In his book *Psychic Power* (formerly *Psionics 101*), Charles Cosimano showed thousands how to build simple, effective and inexpensive radionic devices. Now he's back with a new book that propels radionics into a new decade.

Radionics fuses ancient traditions and modern technology into a workable whole. Cosimano shows how radionic devices can be used for such tasks as

- Measuring the aura
- Controlling functions of the chakras
- Thought control
- Self-defense

The author also includes brand-new diagrams for psychic amplifiers and plans for a crystal transmitter. *Psionic Power* offers readers fascinating insight into techniques of chakra balancing, healing, psychic self-defense and more.

0-87542-096-6, 214 pgs., mass market, illus.   **$3.95**

LIFE FORCE
by Leo Ludzia

A secret living energy—as ancient as the Pyramids, as modern as Star Wars. Since the beginning of time, certain people have known that there *is* this energy—a power that can be used by people for healing, magick, and spiritual development. It's been called many names: Mana, Orgone, Psionic, Prana, Kundalini, Odic force, Chi and others.

Leo Ludzia puts it all together in this amazing book *Life Force*. This is the first book which shows the histories and compares the theories and methods of *using* this marvelous energy. This *Force* is available to us all, if only we know how to tap into it. Ludzia shows you how to make devices which will help you better use and generate this *Life Force*. This specialized information includes easy-to-follow-directions on how to build and use pyramids and Orgone Generators such as those used by Wilhelm Reich, and how to make and use the "Black Box" designed and used by the genius inventor T.G. Hieronymus.

0-87542-437-6, 220 pgs., mass market, illus.   **$3.95**

PSYCHIC POWER
by Charles Cosimano

Although popular in many parts of the world, *Radionics* machines have had little application in America, *UNTIL NOW! Psychic Power* introduces these machines to America with a new purpose: to increase your psychic powers!

Using the easy, step-by-step instructions, and for less than a $10.00 investment, you can build a machine which will allow you to read other people's minds, influence their thoughts, communicate with their dreams and be more successful when you do divinations such as working with Tarot cards or Pendulums.

For thousands of years, people have looked for an easy, simple and sure way to increase their psychic abilities. Now, the science of psionics allows you to do just that! This book is practical, fun and an excellent source for those wishing to achieve results with etheric energies.

0-87542-097-4, 224 pages, mass market, illus. $3.95

HYPNOSIS: A Power Program for Self-Improvement
by William Hewitt

There is no other hypnosis book on the market that has the depth, scope, and explicit detail as does this book. The exact and complete wording of dozens of hypnosis routines is given. Real case histories and examples are included for a broad spectrum of situations. Precise instructions for achieving self-hypnosis, the alpha state, and theta state are given. There are dozens of hypnotic suggestions given covering virtually any type of situation one might encounter. The book tells how to become a professional hypnotist. It tells how to become expert at self-hypnosis all by yourself without external help. And it even contains a short dissertation going "beyond hypnosis" into the realm of psychic phenomena. There is something of value here for nearly everyone.

This book details exactly how to gain all you want—to enrich your life at every level. No matter how simple or how profound your goals, this book teaches you how to realize them. The book is not magic; it is a powerful key to unlock the magic within each of us.

0-87542-300-0, 192 pgs., 5¼ x 8, softcover $6.95

THE ART OF SPIRITUAL HEALING
by Keith Sherwood

Each of you has the potential to be a healer; to heal yourself and to become a channel for healing others. Healing energy is always flowing through you. Learn how to recognize and tap this incredible energy source. You do not need to be a victim of disease or poor health. Rid yourself of negativity and become a channel for positive healing.

Become acquainted with your three auras and learn how to recognize problems and heal them on a higher level before they become manifested in the physical body as disease.

Special techniques make this book a "breakthrough" to healing power, but you are also given a concise, easy-to-follow regimen of good health to follow in order to maintain a superior state of being. This is a practical guide to healing.

0-87542-720-0, 224 pgs., 5¼ x 8, illus., softcover $7.95

CHAKRA THERAPY
by Keith Sherwood

Keith Sherwood presents another excellent how-to book on healing. His previous book, *The Art of Spiritual Healing*, has helped many people learn how to heal themselves and others.

Chakra Therapy follows in the same direction: Understand yourself, know how your body and mind function, and learn how to overcome negative programming so that you can become a free, healthy, self-fulfilled human being.

This book fills in the missing pieces of the human anatomy system left out by orthodox psychological models. It serves as a superb workbook. Within its pages are exercises and techniques designed to increase your level of energy, to transmute unhealthy frequencies of energy into healthy ones, to bring you back into balance and harmony with your self, your loved ones and the multidimensional world you live in. Finally, it will help bring you back into union with the universal field of energy and consciousness.

Chakra Therapy will teach you how to heal yourself by healing your energy system because it is actually energy in its myriad forms which determines a person's physical, emotional and mental health.

0-87542-721-9, 270 pgs., 5¼ x 8, illus., softcover $7.95

THE LLEWELLYN PRACTICAL GUIDE
TO CREATIVE VISUALIZATION
by Denning & Phillips

All things you will ever want must have their start in your mind. The average person uses very little of the full creative power that is his, potentially. It's like the power locked in the atom—it's all there, but you have to learn to release it and apply it constructively.

IF YOU CAN SEE IT ... in your Mind's Eye ... you will have it! It's true: you can have whatever you want—but there are "laws" to mental creation that must be followed.

Through an easy series of step-by-step, progressive exercises, your mind is applied to bring desire into realization! Wealth, power, success, happiness ... psychic powers ... even what we call magickal power and spiritual attainment ... all can be yours. You can easily develop this completely natural power, and correctly apply it, for your immediate and practical benefit. Illustrated with unique, "puts-you-into-the-picture" visualization aids.

0-87542-183-0, 304 pgs., 5¼ x 8, illus., softcover $7.95

THE LLEWELLYN PRACTICAL GUIDE
TO PSYCHIC SELF-DEFENSE AND WELL-BEING
by Denning & Phillips

Psychic well-being and Psychic self-defense are two sides of the same coin—just as physical health and resistance to disease are: each person (and every living thing) is surrounded by an electro-magnetic force field, or AURA, that can provide the means to psychic self-defense and to dynamic well-being. This book explores the world of very real "psychic warfare" that we all are victims of.

This book shows the nature of genuine psychic attacks—ranging from actual acts of black magic to bitter jealousy and hate—and the reality of psychic stress, the structure of the psyche and its interrelationship with the physical body. It shows how each person must develop his weakened aura into a powerful defense-shield—thereby gaining both physical protection and energetic well-being that can extend to protection from physical violence, accidents ... even ill health.

0-87542-190-3, 306 pgs., 5¼ x 8, illus., softcover $7.95

THE SECRET OF LETTING GO
by Guy Finley

Whether you need to let go of a painful heartache, a destructive habit, a frightening worry or a nagging discontent, *The Secret of Letting Go* shows you how to call upon your own hidden powers and how they can take you through and beyond any challenge or problem. This book reveals the secret source of a brand-new kind of inner strength. In the light of your new and higher self-understanding, emotional difficulties such as loneliness, fear, anxiety and frustration fade into nothingness as you happily discover they never really existed in the first place. With a foreword by Desi Arnaz, Jr., and introduction by Dr. Jesse Freeland, *The Secret of Letting Go* is a pleasing balance of questions and answers, illustrative examples, truth tales, and stimulating dialogues that allow the reader to share in the exciting discoveries that lead up to lasting self-liberation. This is a book for the discriminating, intelligent, and sensitive reader who is looking for *real* answers.

0-87542-223-3, 220 pgs., 51/4 × 8, softcover $9.95

BEYOND HYPNOSIS
by William Hewitt

This book contains a complete system for using hypnosis to enter a beneficial altered state of consciousness in order to develop your psychic abilities. Here is a 30-day program (just 10-20 minutes per day) to release your psychic awareness and then hone it to a fine skill through a series of mental exercises that anyone can do!

Beyond Hypnosis lets you make positive changes in your life. You will find yourself doing things that you only dreamed about in the past: out-of-body experiences, including previously secret instructions to easily and safely leave your body. Learn channeling, where you will easily be able to communicate with spiritual, nonphysical entities. With skill improvement, you will learn techniques to improve your physical or mental abilities. Speed up your learning and reading abilities and yet retain more of the information you study. A must for students of all kinds!

Beyond Hypnosis shows you how to create your own reality, how to reshape your own life and the lives of others—and ultimately how to reshape the world and beyond what we call this world! This book will introduce you to a beneficial altered state of consciousness which is achieved by using your own natural abilities to control your mind. It is in this state where you will learn to expand your psychic abilities beyond belief!

0-87542-305-1, 224 pgs., 51/4 x 8, softcover $7.95

CRYSTAL HEALING: The Next Step
by Phyllis Galde

Discover the further secrets of quartz crystal! Now modern research and use have shown that crystals have even more healing and therapeutic properties than has been realized. Learn why polished, smoothed crystal is better to use for heightening your intuition, improving creativity and healing.

Learn to use crystals for reprogramming your subconscious to eliminate problems and negative attitudes that prevent success. Here are techniques that people have successfully used—not just theories.

This book reveals newly discovered abilities of crystal now accessible to all, and is a sensible approach to crystal use. *Crystal Healing* will be your guide to improve the quality of your life and expand your consciousness.

0-87542-246-2, 224 pgs., mass market, illus. $3.95

CRYSTAL SPIRIT
by Michael G. Smith

Crystal Spirit is the book thousands of people have asked for after reading the popular *Crystal Power* by the same author. Now that the fad appeal of crystals is wearing off, we can use crystals to experience the deeper essence of ourselves—to facilitate our self-awareness, self-growth, and self-understanding.

Crystal Spirit contains timely and hard-to-find information on:

* New types of crystal rods
* Crystal pyramid devices
* The crystal pipe from Native American traditions
* Ki and Chi energy through crystals for martial artists
* Health and exercise with crystal wristbands

The book begins with explanations of crystals of the ancient past and how to reconstruct your own: the Trident Krystallos, Atlantean Crystal Cross, Crux Crystallum. The book ends with the introduction of the new crystal pipe based on traditional Native American practices and the science of Universal Energy. Between these two chapters is a wealth of information and instruction on other crystal inventions.

0-87542-726-X, 208 pgs., mass market, illus. $3.95